NATIONAL ACADEMIES *Sciences Engineering Medicine*

NATIONAL ACADEMIES PRESS
Washington, DC

Development, Implementation, and Evaluation of Community-Based Suicide Prevention Grants Programs

Convened April 29, 2025

Tina M. Winters, *Rapporteur*

Board on Behavioral, Cognitive, and Sensory Sciences

Division of Behavioral and Social Sciences and Education

Proceedings of a Workshop

NATIONAL ACADEMIES PRESS 500 Fifth Street, NW Washington, DC 20001

This activity was supported by a contract between the National Academy of Sciences and the Department of Veterans Affairs (#36C24524C0125). Any opinions, findings, conclusions, or recommendations expressed in this publication do not necessarily reflect the views of any organization or agency that provided support for the project.

International Standard Book Number-13: 978-0-309-99520-7
Digital Object Identifier: https://doi.org/10.17226/29215

This publication is available from the National Academies Press, 500 Fifth Street, NW, Keck 360, Washington, DC 20001; (800) 624-6242; https://nap.nationalacademies.org.

The manufacturer's authorized representative in the European Union for product safety is Authorised Rep Compliance Ltd., Ground Floor, 71 Lower Baggot Street, Dublin D02 P593 Ireland; www.arccompliance.com.

Copyright 2025 by the National Academy of Sciences. National Academies of Sciences, Engineering, and Medicine and National Academies Press and the graphical logos for each are all trademarks of the National Academy of Sciences. All rights reserved.

Printed in the United States of America.

Suggested citation: National Academies of Sciences, Engineering, and Medicine. 2025. *Development, Implementation, and Evaluation of Community-Based Suicide Prevention Grants Programs: Proceedings of a Workshop*. Washington, DC: National Academies Press. https://doi.org/10.17226/29215.

The **National Academy of Sciences** was established in 1863 by an Act of Congress, signed by President Lincoln, as a private, nongovernmental institution to advise the nation on issues related to science and technology. Members are elected by their peers for outstanding contributions to research. Dr. Marcia McNutt is president.

The **National Academy of Engineering** was established in 1964 under the charter of the National Academy of Sciences to bring the practices of engineering to advising the nation. Members are elected by their peers for extraordinary contributions to engineering. Dr. Tsu-Jae Liu is president.

The **National Academy of Medicine** (formerly the Institute of Medicine) was established in 1970 under the charter of the National Academy of Sciences to advise the nation on medical and health issues. Members are elected by their peers for distinguished contributions to medicine and health. Dr. Victor J. Dzau is president.

The three Academies work together as the **National Academies of Sciences, Engineering, and Medicine** to provide independent, objective analysis and advice to the nation and conduct other activities to solve complex problems and inform public policy decisions. The National Academies also encourage education and research, recognize outstanding contributions to knowledge, and increase public understanding in matters of science, engineering, and medicine.

Learn more about the National Academies of Sciences, Engineering, and Medicine at **www.nationalacademies.org**.

Consensus Study Reports published by the National Academies of Sciences, Engineering, and Medicine document the evidence-based consensus on the study's statement of task by an authoring committee of experts. Reports typically include findings, conclusions, and recommendations based on information gathered by the committee and the committee's deliberations. Each report has been subjected to a rigorous and independent peer-review process and it represents the position of the National Academies on the statement of task.

Proceedings published by the National Academies of Sciences, Engineering, and Medicine chronicle the presentations and discussions at a workshop, symposium, or other event convened by the National Academies. The statements and opinions contained in proceedings are those of the participants and are not endorsed by other participants, the planning committee, or the National Academies.

Rapid Expert Consultations published by the National Academies of Sciences, Engineering, and Medicine are authored by subject-matter experts on narrowly focused topics that can be supported by a body of evidence. The discussions contained in rapid expert consultations are considered those of the authors and do not contain policy recommendations. Rapid expert consultations are reviewed by the institution before release.

For information about other products and activities of the National Academies, please visit www.nationalacademies.org/about/whatwedo.

WORKSHOP ON BEST PRACTICES FOR IMPLEMENTATION AND EVALUATION OF A NON-CLINICAL COMMUNITY-BASED SUICIDE PREVENTION GRANTS PROGRAM PLANNING COMMITTEE

CARL A. CASTRO (*Chair*), University of Southern California
DIANA E. CLARKE, American Psychiatric Association
DANIEL J. FRIEND, Mathematica
BERNICE A. PESCOSOLIDO, Indiana University Bloomington
ELLYSON R. STOUT, EDC
COLIN G. WALSH, Vanderbilt University

Staff

TINA M. WINTERS, Project Director
SHARON BRITT, Program Coordinator
DANIEL J. WEISS, Director, Board on Behavioral, Cognitive, and Sensory Sciences

Reviewers

This Proceedings of a Workshop was reviewed in draft form by individuals chosen for their diverse perspectives and technical expertise. The purpose of this independent review is to provide candid and critical comments that will assist the National Academies of Sciences, Engineering, and Medicine in making each published proceedings as sound as possible and to ensure that it meets the institutional standards for quality, objectivity, evidence, and responsiveness to the charge. The review comments and draft manuscript remain confidential to protect the integrity of the process.

We thank the following individuals for their review of this proceedings:

LISA BRENNER, University of Colorado Anschutz Medical Campus
GILLY CANTOR, D'Aniello Institute for Veterans and Military Families at Syracuse University
COLLEEN CARR, National Action Alliance for Suicide Prevention
KATRINA MESSER, U.S. VETS

Although the reviewers listed above provided many constructive comments and suggestions, they were not asked to endorse the content of the proceedings nor did they see the final draft before its release. The review of this proceedings was overseen by **NADINE KASLOW,** Emory University School of Medicine. She was responsible for making certain that an independent examination of this proceedings was carried out in accordance with standards of the National Academies and that all review comments were carefully considered. Responsibility for the final content rests entirely with the rapporteur and the National Academies.

Acknowledgments

The Board on Behavioral, Cognitive, and Sensory Sciences expresses its sincere gratitude to the members of the workshop planning committee for their leadership in developing an agenda that supported informative presentations and rich discussions. The Board also thanks the invited speakers, whose expertise and thoughtful engagement made the workshop a success. We are deeply grateful for the generous support of the U.S. Department of Veterans Affairs (VA), and to VA Office of Suicide Prevention staff members Bruce Crow, Sandra Foley, Melissa Hall, and Michelle Kuntz for their collaboration and guidance throughout the planning process.

The Board also wishes to thank Sharon Britt for her invaluable contributions to the coordination and execution of this project; Bea Porter for her careful edit of the proceedings, as well as her contributions to Chapter 5 and the publication process; Kirsten Sampson Snyder for her oversight and guidance during the review and publication process; and Anthony Janifer for his support during the review process.

Contents

Acronyms and Abbreviations — xvii

1 **Introduction** — 1
WORKSHOP GOALS AND INTRODUCTORY
   PERSPECTIVES, 1
ORGANIZATION OF THIS PROCEEDINGS, 4
REFERENCES, 5

2 **Setting the Stage: Examples of Non-Clinical Community-Based Suicide Prevention Programs** — 7
USAA FACE THE FIGHT INITIATIVE, 7
   Face the Fight Structure and Collaborative Model, 8
   Face the Fight Impact and Data-Driven Strategy, 9
   Examples of Funded Activities, 13
VIRGINIA DEPARTMENT OF VETERANS SERVICES
   SUICIDE PREVENTION AND OPIOID ADDICTION
   SERVICES PROGRAM, 13
   Program Launch and Growth, 14
   Grantee Diversity and Impact, 14
WHITE MOUNTAIN APACHE CELEBRATING LIFE
   SUICIDE PREVENTION PROGRAM, 17
   Tribal Context and Early Response to Suicide, 18
   The Celebrating Life Surveillance and Case Management
      System, 18
   Celebrating Life Program Impact, 19

GARRETT LEE SMITH AND NATIVE CONNECTIONS
SUICIDE PREVENTION PROGRAMS, 21
Origin and Structure of the GLS Program, 22
Evaluation Findings, Impact, and Program Reach, 23
Native Connections Program, 23
REFERENCES, 26

3   Considerations for Program Development and Oversight and
    Grantee-Level Implementation and Performance Metrics   27
    FOUNDATIONAL PRESENTATIONS, 28
        Theory of Change, Theory of Action, and Performance
            Metrics, 28
        The Public Health Approach and Comprehensive Suicide
            Prevention, 30
        Models for Effective Community Suicide Prevention, 37
        Developing Logic Models for Community-Based Suicide
            Prevention, 40
        Comprehensive Technical Assistance to Support Program
            Outcomes, 41
        Design of Actionable Dashboards for Supporting Program
            Implementation and Oversight, 47
    PANEL DISCUSSIONS AND AUDIENCE Q&A, 49
        Lessons Learned from Examples of Non-Clinical
            Community-Based Suicide Prevention Efforts, 51
        Expert Insights on Program Development and Oversight
            and Grantee-Level Implementation and Performance
            Metrics, 57
        Audience Q&A, 63
    REFERENCES, 65

4   Considerations for Program Evaluation   67
    LESSONS LEARNED AND EXAMPLES FROM THE FIELD, 67
        From Program Evaluation to Comprehensive, Community-
            Based Suicide Prevention Evaluation: Lessons Learned
            from the Field, 67
        Multi-Site Community-Based Suicide Prevention Program
            Evaluation: An Example from the Field, 71
    PANEL DISCUSSION AND AUDIENCE Q&A, 73
        Evolution of Program Design and Administration Based on
            Evaluation Findings, 73
        Best Practices for Balancing Evaluation Across Multiple
            Levels, 75

Using Intermediate Indicators to Track Progress Toward
Suicide Prevention Goals, 76
Grantee Involvement in Evaluation and Building and
Sustaining Capacity Over Time, 78
Audience Q&A, 79

5 **Communicating Program Results**   83
STRATEGIC COMMUNICATION AND DATA
STORYTELLING, 83
Best Processes for Strategic Communication of Program
Results, 84
Data Storytelling: Best Practices for Communicating
Impact, 89
PANEL DISCUSSION AND AUDIENCE Q&A, 95
Tailoring Communication to Different Audiences, 95
Evaluating Communication Strategies, 98
Sharing Academic Literature Effectively, 99
Audience Q&A, 100
REFERENCES, 102

6 **Reflections on Workshop Themes**   103
PROGRAM DESIGN, 103
PROGRAM IMPLEMENTATION, 104
PROGRAM EVALUATION, 104
DEFINING AND COMMUNICATING SUCCESS, 104
CONCLUSION, 105

Appendix A Workshop Agenda   107

Appendix B Biosketches   113

Box, Figures, and Tables

BOX

1-1 Statement of Task, 2

FIGURES

2-1 Visualizing Face the Fight's impact, 10
2-2 Centers for Disease Control and Prevention (CDC) evidence-informed strategies and dynamic data modeling, 11
2-3 Virginia Department of Veterans Services Suicide Prevention and Opioid Addiction Services (SOS) Community Grant first year outcomes, 15
2-4 Screening tools used by Virginia Department of Veteran Services Suicide Prevention and Opioid Addiction Services (SOS) grantees, 16
2-5 Suicide attempts and deaths among the White Mountain Apache Tribe, 20
2-6 Suicide death rates for U.S. youth ages 10–24, by race, 21
2-7 Impact of Garrett Lee Smith (GLS) programming by duration of exposure, 24
2-8 Map of Garrett Lee Smith (GLS) state and tribal grantees, FY 2021, 25

3-1 Psychoeducational resilience-building workshop as an illustrative example of a cohesive theory of change, 29
3-2 Why do performance measurement?, 29

3-3	Public health approach to suicide prevention, 31
3-4	Suicide rates by age group and sex, 1999 versus 2023, 32
3-5	Suicide rates by race and ethnicity and sex, 1999 versus 2023, 33
3-6	Veteran and non-veteran suicide rates, 2001 to 2022, 34
3-7	Scope of suicide-related thoughts and behaviors among U.S. adults, 2021, 35
3-8	Illustrative model for suicide prevention across the continuum of risk, 37
3-9	What to implement for effective community suicide prevention: Suicide Prevention Resource Center (SPRC) comprehensive approach, 39
3-10	How to do effective community suicide prevention: Suicide Prevention Resource Center (SPRC) strategic planning approach, 39
3-11	Logic model layout and terminology, 42
3-12	Logic model development and example, 43
3-13	Comprehensive technical assistance example, 46
3-14	Data dashboard actionability, 48
3-15	Actionability as a design process, 50
4-1	Nested evaluation model for suicide prevention, 69
4-2	Principles of participatory evaluation in community-based suicide prevention, 71
5-1	The COM-B model of planning behavioral interventions and a "typical" logic model of the policy process, 85
5-2	Think about the desired outcome and work backward to develop communication strategies, 87
5-3	Crafting a narrative: Mapping data storytelling to a classic story arc using context, characters, climb, consequence, and conclusion, 91
5-4	Types of visualization: Examples of tools to communicate quantitative and qualitative data, 92
5-5	Quantitative "before and after," 93
5-6	Qualitative "before and after," 94

TABLES

2-1	Comparison of the Grant-Making Components of the Garrett Lee Smith (GLS) Program, 22
3-1	Comprehensive Suicide Prevention Strategies and Approaches, 36

Acronyms and Abbreviations

AFSP American Foundation for Suicide Prevention

BCBT-SP Brief Cognitive Behavioral Therapy for Suicide Prevention

CDC Centers for Disease Control and Prevention
CRP Crisis Response Planning
C-SSRS Columbia-Suicide Severity Rating Scale

EDC Education Development Center
ERIF Early Identification Referral Form

Fox SPGP Sergent Parker Gordon Fox Suicide Prevention Grant Program

GLS Garrett Lee Smith

NRA National Rifle Association

SAMHSA Substance Abuse and Mental Health Services Administration
SMVF service members, veterans, and their families
SOS Virginia Department of Veterans Services Suicide Prevention and Opioid Addiction Services program
SPRC Suicide Prevention Resource Center

UT Health San Antonio	University of Texas Health San Antonio
VA	U.S. Department of Veterans Affairs

1

Introduction

This proceedings presents a summary of what occurred at the Workshop on Best Practices for Implementation and Evaluation of a Non-Clinical Community-Based Suicide Prevention Grants Program, a hybrid workshop[1] hosted on April 29, 2025, by the National Academies of Sciences, Engineering, and Medicine's (National Academies) Board on Behavioral, Cognitive, and Sensory Sciences (see Box 1-1 for the Statement of Task and Appendix A for the workshop agenda). The workshop was sponsored by the U.S. Department of Veterans Affairs (VA), and the National Academies appointed a workshop planning committee to organize and convene the workshop (see Appendix B for biographical sketches). This proceedings was prepared by the workshop rapporteur; the views contained in the proceedings are those of individual workshop participants and do not necessarily represent the views of all workshop participants, the planning committee, or the National Academies.

WORKSHOP GOALS AND INTRODUCTORY PERSPECTIVES

Workshop presentations and discussions were structured to address the following topics as they pertain to non-clinical, community-based suicide prevention grants programs:

---

[1] To view the workshop recording, visit https://www.nationalacademies.org/event/48866_04-2025_best-practices-for-implementation-and-evaluation-of-a-suicide-prevention-grants-programs-a-workshop

- Program development and oversight,
- Grantee-level implementation and performance metrics,
- Program evaluation, and
- Communicating program results.

In keeping with the Statement of Task (Box 1-1), the overall focus of the workshop was on non-clinical community-based programs intended to mitigate the impacts of social determinants of health on suicide risk. As discussed in the proceedings for an earlier workshop convened for the VA, social determinants of health include socioeconomic factors, social supports, health behaviors, exposure to violence, and characteristics of the physical environments in which individuals live and work (National Academies, 2022). Across workshop discussions, speakers often used the term "upstream risk factors"; while this is not precisely synonymous with social determinants of health, it does reflect many of the components of social determinants of health. In addition, a few workshop speakers touched on clinical interventions due to the importance of referring individuals experiencing acute suicidality to appropriate clinical care.

BOX 1-1
Statement of Task

The National Academies of Sciences, Engineering, and Medicine will appoint a planning committee to organize a one-day public workshop followed by a one-day meeting of experts on the best practices for implementation and evaluation of suicide prevention grants programs. The workshop will explore issues, such as the following:

- What are the best practices for initiating a grants program primarily comprised of non-clinical interventions designed to reduce suicide occurrence? How should eligibility for grant recipients be determined and are there effective ways to facilitate a more effective portfolio?
- What are the best practices for evaluating the effectiveness of a grants program designed to mitigate the impacts of social determinants of health on suicide risk and reduce suicide occurrence? What metrics might be employed to demonstrate progress in these areas early in the inception of the program?
- What are best practices for reporting on the effectiveness of a portfolio of grants? How can individual and aggregate data be used to understand the broader population-level impacts? Relatedly, what should the guidelines be for grant recipients in ensuring efficient measurements and data collection, balancing the need for quality and transparency with the burdens of data reporting?

Daniel J. Weiss (National Academies) kicked off the workshop by placing it in the context of earlier convenings sponsored by the VA Office of Suicide Prevention that were overseen by the Board on Behavioral, Cognitive, and Sensory Sciences pointing participants to the resulting publications: *Community Interventions to Prevent Veteran Suicide: Proceedings of a Virtual Symposium* (National Academies, 2022) and *Identifying and Managing Veteran Suicide Risk: Proceedings of a Workshop* (National Academies, 2023). Weiss remarked on the importance of the board's efforts in support of the Office of Suicide Prevention and the people who have served our country. Carl A. Castro (Col., U.S. Army-ret; Suzanne Dworak-Peck School of Social Work, University of Southern California; chair, workshop planning committee) echoed Weiss's emphasis on the importance of the topic for both the active duty and veteran communities.

To frame the day's discussions, Matthew Miller (VA Office of Suicide Prevention) offered an overview of veteran suicide trends and the core principles guiding the VA's Staff Sergeant Parker Gordon Fox Suicide Prevention Grant Program (Fox SPGP). He began by highlighting several encouraging indicators of progress in reducing veteran suicide, citing the most recent available data from 2022. That year's suicide count was lower than 12 of the previous 14 years. Over 20 years, the suicide rate among veterans has risen more slowly than that of the non-veteran U.S. adult population. In 2022, the suicide rate for male veterans increased by 1.6 percent, compared to a 1.8 percent increase among non-veteran adult males; for non-veteran adult females the suicide rate increased by 5 percent, while the rate for female veterans decreased by 24 percent.

Miller also pointed to notable progress across subpopulations within the veteran community. Among veterans diagnosed with mental health conditions—who typically face elevated suicide risk—there have been reductions in suicide rates over time. For example, across 20 years, the suicide rate decreased by more than 30 percent for veterans diagnosed with a mood disorder and receiving care through the Veterans Health Administration. Similar reductions were observed among veterans diagnosed with post-traumatic stress disorder. For veterans with anxiety disorders, and substance use disorders, there has been a 20 percent decrease in the suicide rate over this period.

Miller described how the Fox SPGP, launched in 2022, embodies three foundational principles that guide the VA's suicide prevention efforts:

1. *Suicide is preventable; it is not inevitable.* Interventions at the individual, community, and population levels can effectively reduce suicide risk and save lives.
2. *Suicide prevention requires a public health approach.* While high-quality clinical care—including emergency services and integrated

primary and mental health care—is essential, it is not sufficient on its own. Many risk and protective factors for suicide exist outside of the clinical setting. Addressing these factors through a public health framework is essential, and this is the core focus of the Fox SPGP.
3. ***Everyone has a role to play.*** Veteran suicide prevention requires contributions from many stakeholders outside of the VA. The Fox SPGP supports this by investing in community-based approaches and augmenting existing local resources that serve veterans. The goal is to equip, support, and expand the work being done in communities to prevent veteran suicide.

Miller reported positive developments from the first three years of the Fox SPGP. A congressionally mandated report after the program's first year offered useful early insights into program start-up, reach, and operational dynamics, though it was limited in its ability to assess outcomes. A more recent third-party evaluation described encouraging indicators of progress in key areas, including program scope, participant outreach, and linkage to care. It also highlighted the program's success in connecting veterans with both VA and community-based services—particularly emergency mental health resources.

Miller emphasized the VA's commitment to ongoing improvement, learning, and collaboration. He described the workshop as a valuable opportunity to engage with the broader suicide prevention and mental health community—to gain insights, solicit feedback, and identify ways to strengthen both the Fox SPGP and broader VA efforts.

Looking ahead, Miller expressed optimism about the continuation of the Fox SPGP, citing sustained momentum, promising early results, and congressional support. He also noted the VA's broader interest in contributing to the field of suicide prevention beyond its immediate mission. In addition to saving veteran lives, the VA sees its role as advancing knowledge that benefits suicide prevention efforts across the U.S. adult population more broadly.

ORGANIZATION OF THIS PROCEEDINGS

The organization of this proceedings reflects the structure of the workshop, with each chapter corresponding to a major session. Chapter 2 summarizes presentations on examples of non-clinical community-based suicide prevention programs, which were featured early in the workshop to establish context for the sessions that followed. Chapter 3 addresses two interrelated topics—considerations for program development and oversight, and grantee-level implementation and performance metrics—which were covered in a single session due to their natural overlap and the continuity of discussion. Chapters 4 and 5 describe the final two workshop sessions, which focused on considerations for the evaluation of community-based suicide prevention programs and the communication of program results, respectively. These were treated as distinct sessions to allow for more focused and in-depth exploration. Chapter 6 offers reflections on themes and key takeaway messages from the workshop.

REFERENCES

National Academies of Sciences, Engineering, and Medicine (National Academies). (2022). *Community interventions to prevent veteran suicide: The role of social determinants. Proceedings of a virtual symposium.* The National Academies Press. https://doi.org/10.17226/26638

———. (2023). *Identifying and managing veteran suicide risk Proceedings of a workshop.* The National Academies Press. https://doi.org/10.17226/27195

2

Setting the Stage: Examples of Non-Clinical Community-Based Suicide Prevention Programs

Following the opening session, the workshop turned to presentations on five programs that provide support for non-clinical community-based suicide prevention efforts. These presentations were designed to frame later sessions and ground them in real-world experience. Providing detailed overviews of their programs ahead of in-depth sessions on program oversight, implementation, and evaluation, as well as communication of program results, allowed attendees to better understand the context for the contributions of these program leaders as panelists in those later sessions—particularly how program characteristics such as setting, population served, duration, and infrastructure shaped their insights on the topics at hand. The programs described varied in size, scope, and length of time in operation, thus offering diverse perspectives on challenges, innovations, and lessons applicable across community-based suicide prevention efforts.

USAA FACE THE FIGHT INITIATIVE

David Rozek (Associate Professor, Department of Psychiatry and Behavioral Sciences, University of Texas Health San Antonio [UT Health San Antonio] and Senior Scientific Advisor for the Face the Fight initiative) provided an overview of Face the Fight, which was officially launched in 2023. He stated that it was founded by USAA, the Humana Foundation, and Reach Resilience to bring together veteran-serving organizations, foundations, non-profits, corporations, and others interested in joining the effort to pool resources and expertise for raising awareness and supporting veteran suicide prevention. Face the Fight is dedicated to expanding access to and availability of evidence-based, proven suicide prevention programs with the overarching mission of making a measurable, lasting reduction in veteran suicide rates, Rozek added.

Face the Fight Structure and Collaborative Model

Rozek described the three core components of the Face the Fight initiative:

1. **Public Awareness Campaign**—An ongoing national effort to reduce stigma and promote awareness of resources for veteran suicide prevention.
2. **Coalition Engagement**—A network of more than 250 organizations committed to taking meaningful actions, making sustained commitments, and collaborating across sectors to reduce veteran suicide.
3. **Grant-making**—Strategic investments aimed at scaling evidence-informed interventions for suicide prevention and responding quickly to emerging needs.

He emphasized that the initiative is designed to leverage the strengths of every partner. While many coalition members do not have veteran suicide prevention as their primary mission, they bring valuable expertise, networks, and resources to advance the shared goal.

Face the Fight's success relies on the coordinated efforts of the founding partners and key strategic partners, each contributing unique capabilities to the initiative, Rozek explained. The founding partners, USAA, Humana Foundation, and Reach Resilience, have developed an executive committee of key supporters to oversee Face the Fight. He added that USAA also uses internal staff and resources to provide foundational support that enables Face the Fight to operate effectively.

UT Health San Antonio, a strategic partner in the Face the Fight initiative, serves as the initiative's day-to-day scientific advisor, providing research oversight, ensuring initiatives remain evidence based, and integrating emerging best practices, Rozek stated. This work also includes guiding the grant-making process to ensure grantees are implementing proven suicide prevention programs and continuing to gather important data to advance the science. In this capacity, Rozek continued, it co-leads the Scientific Advisory Committee, a group of multi-disciplinary experts who provide guidance on suicide prevention strategies and help shape the direction of Face the Fight.

Rozek noted that UT Health San Antonio also manages the technical assistance process for grantees. The technical assistance process starts before a grant is awarded, he explained; the team works with prospective grantees to understand their infrastructure and needs, and how they can help the organization build, scale, or integrate evidence-informed suicide prevention practices. During the grant period, the technical assistance team meets with grantees at least monthly to support efforts toward long-term scalability and sustainability. A major goal, Rozek stated, is to promote program sustainability so that grantees do not face a "funding cliff," where the conclusion of Face the Fight support would also mean the end of their programming.

Rozek added that the Elizabeth Dole Foundation brings considerable experience in running coalitions, so drawing on their expertise for leading the coalition enables Face the Fight to maximize the return on participation for coalition members. The Foundation also leads communications and engagement efforts, connecting both coalition members and broader audiences to the mission. Rozek stressed that across all components and partnerships, Face the Fight aims to remain flexible, nimble, and responsive to evolving needs in the veteran suicide prevention landscape.

Face the Fight Impact and Data-Driven Strategy

Rozek highlighted aspects of Face the Fight's impact to date, as illustrated in Figure 2-1. He noted the Face the Fight coalition includes over 200 members, many of whom are non-profit veteran-serving organizations, as well as government liaisons. Their scientific advisory group is comprised of 32 members with diverse areas of expertise. The advisory group has held several listening sessions with veterans and veteran families and has collected significant feedback to ensure they understand the landscape, including problems that are sometimes missed, he added. Based on dynamic data modeling (explained below), the initiative is projected to have saved 6,500 lives by 2032.

Face the Fight–supported programs have screened 245,000 veterans for suicide risk using tools such as the Columbia-Suicide Severity Rating Scale (C-SSRS; Posner et al., 2011) in both clinical and community settings, Rozek shared. They have also delivered suicide-specific, evidence-informed interventions, including Brief Cognitive Behavioral Therapy for Suicide Prevention (BCBT-SP) and Crisis Response Planning (CRP; Bryan & Rudd, 2018), to 39,000 veterans; trained over 800 clinicians on suicide-specific interventions (e.g., BCBT-SP, CRP); and engaged in over 12,000 conversations about secure firearms storage.

Rozek noted that Face the Fight takes a public health approach that is aligned with evidence-informed focus areas of the Centers for Disease Control and Prevention (CDC) model (see Figure 2-2). Currently, Face the Fight focuses on the first three areas of the model in their grant-making:

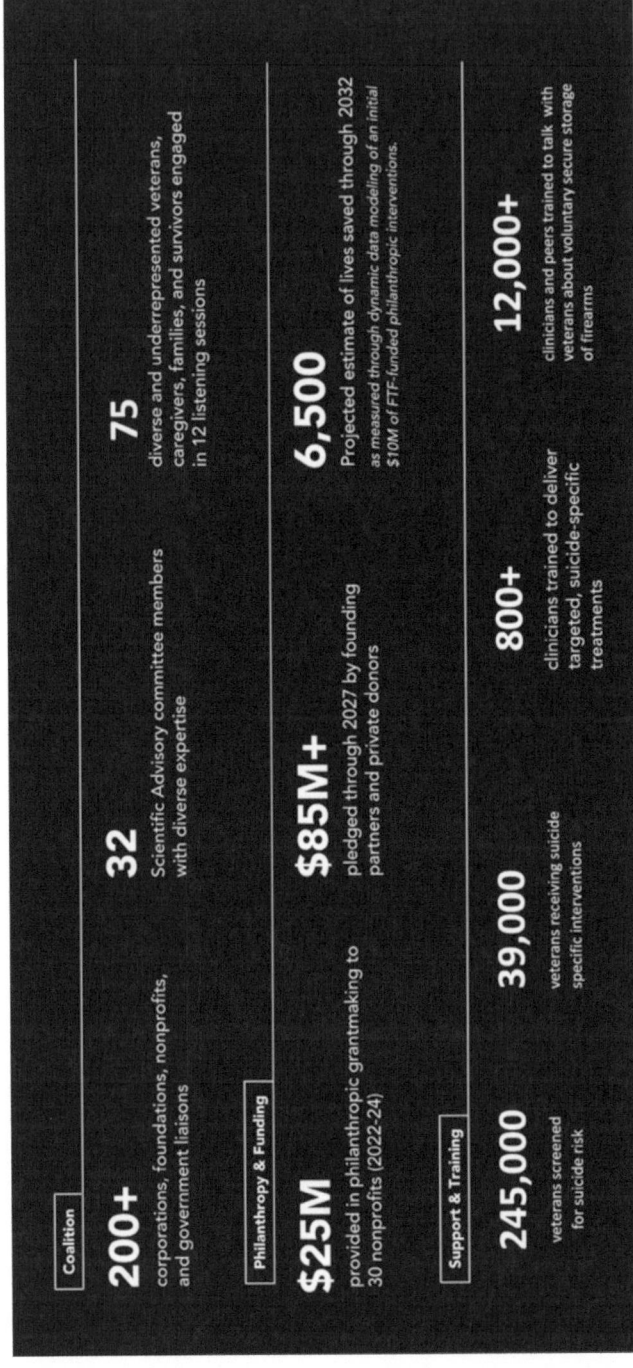

FIGURE 2-1 Visualizing Face the Fight's impact.
SOURCE: Presented by David Rozek on April 29, 2025.

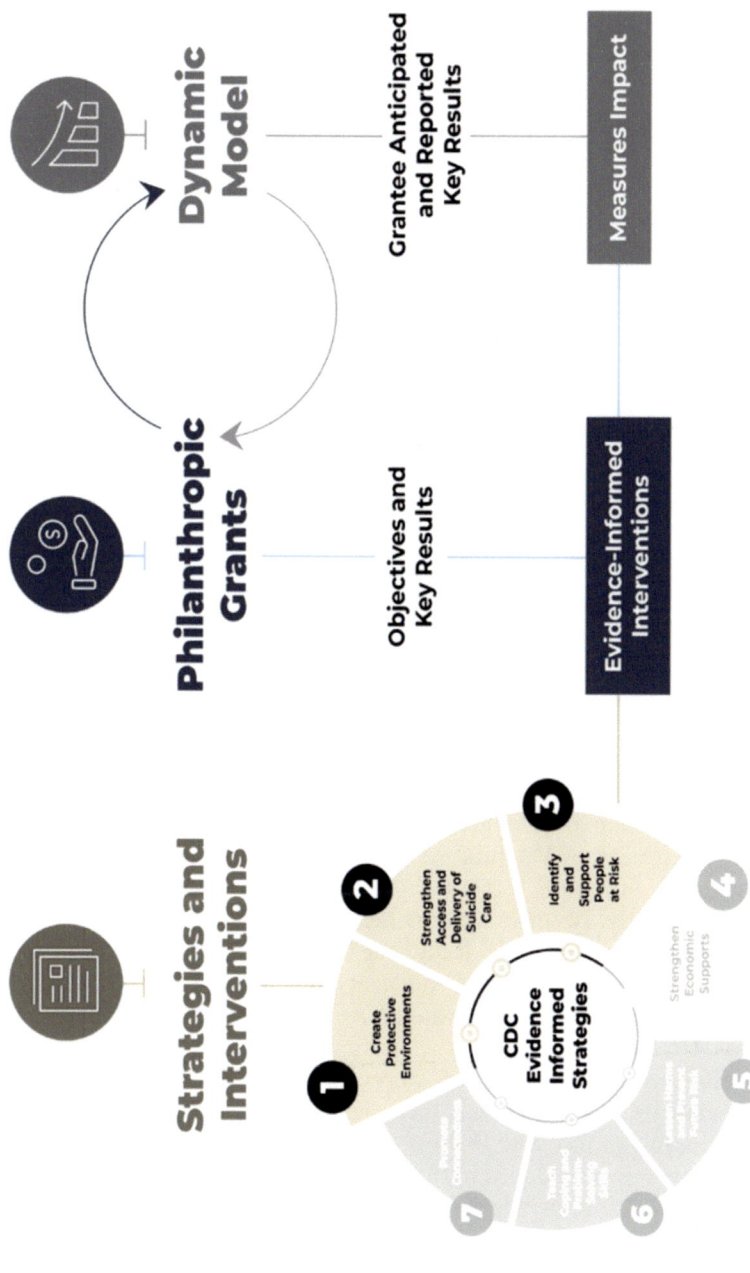

FIGURE 2-2 Centers for Disease Control and Prevention (CDC) evidence-informed strategies and dynamic data modeling.
SOURCE: Presented by David Rozek on April 29, 2025.

1. Create protective environments,
2. Strengthen access and delivery of suicide-specific care, and
3. Identify and support people at risk.

Rozek added that they plan to expand to the other four areas as the initiative matures.

To measure impacts, Face the Fight uses a dynamic data modeling strategy adapted from a model developed by the American Foundation for Suicide Prevention as part of the Bold Goal,[1] Rozek reported. Dynamic data modeling is a well-established decision-support tool to guide investments and actions to address complex public health issues like suicide. The approach

- Supports systems and public health approaches,
- Informs strategic decision-making,
- Supports measurement of progress,
- Offers flexibility, and
- Allows for adjustments in real time.

The model allows for scenario testing of scaling interventions to guide decisions about the most effective and impactful grant-making activities, Rozek explained. When thinking about providing grant funding, Face the Fight uses their dynamic data model to estimate how much impact the grant or organization will have—projecting the number of lives saved that they believe that grant will have. This also allows for planning in grant-making and ensuring that a more holistic and less siloed approach to funding occurs to maximize the impact of the funding portfolio, he noted.

Rozek stated that data collected from grantees, combined with data from the Department of Veterans Affairs (VA) and information from the relevant scientific literature, is regularly incorporated into the model, which is updated frequently. To illustrate how the model functions, he presented a simplified hypothetical example. If all Face the Fight–funded programs and interventions were turned off, the model would mirror the baseline rates reported in the *Veteran Suicide Prevention Annual Report* (U.S. Department of Veterans Affairs, 2024b). In this scenario, with 10,000 highly distressed veterans, the model would project approximately 700 suicide attempts and 70 deaths by suicide. Rozek then described a scenario in which a hypothetical intervention with a 50 percent effectiveness rate in reducing suicide attempts was introduced in the model. If all 10,000 veterans were to receive the intervention, the model would project a 50 percent reduction in

---

[1] The American Foundation for Suicide Prevention has taken on the Bold Goal to reduce the U.S. suicide rate by 20 percent by 2025. See https://afsp.org/the-bold-goal/

both suicide attempts and, in turn, suicide deaths, resulting in an estimated 35 lives saved. He emphasized that the actual model is significantly more complex, as different interventions have different levels of effectiveness and impact. Additionally, some individuals may receive multiple interventions, and the system accounts for interaction effects through integrated pipelines. As more data become available, Rozek added, the team will continue refining and validating different components of the dynamic model.

Examples of Funded Activities

Rozek highlighted two activities funded by Face the Fight. The first activity he described is the Pause to Protect initiative at the University of Colorado, which is working with five local retailers selling secure storage for firearms and investigating how much of a discount it takes to have veterans want to purchase some sort of secure storage. Face the Fight is examining how this intervention might be implemented nationally with corporate sponsors in a larger scale where couponing might be available across the country. The second activity highlighted by Rozek is an initiative at the Robert Irvine Foundation. Robert Irvine, a chef, was interested in using the power of food to bring people together in support of suicide prevention. The Face the Fight initiative helped the organization to think about how to bring peer-based and community-based response CRP and lethal means safety conversations into an effort that reaches many thousands of veterans in a more approachable and less clinical environment than is typical for these interventions.

Rozek concluded by noting that the ultimate goals of the Face the Fight initiative are to ensure grantees work across their coalition so that there is cross-pollination of ideas and practices, to think about scale and sustainability, and to measure outcomes over time.

VIRGINIA DEPARTMENT OF VETERANS SERVICES SUICIDE PREVENTION AND OPIOID ADDICTION SERVICES PROGRAM

Brandi Jancaitis (Director, Virginia Veteran and Family Support Program, Virginia Department of Veterans Services) opened by reflecting on her dual perspective as both a public servant and a military family member. Her presentation highlighted the challenges and successes of rapidly developing a statewide infrastructure for suicide prevention and opioid addiction services aimed at supporting service members, veterans, and their families (SMVF) in Virginia.

The Virginia Department of Veterans Services Suicide Prevention and Opioid Addiction Services (SOS) program officially launched in July 2022, with a legislative mandate to address the problems of veteran suicide and opioid addiction. Staff was tasked with putting together a best practices program and building a grant-making program within a year of the launch. Jancaitis likened this challenge to justifying the existence of the airport while building it and flying the plane simultaneously.

Program Launch and Growth

The SOS program has awarded $12.7 million to 59 community grantees, some of whom are finishing their second year of activity. The program also has eight research grantees who have been awarded nearly $1.65 million. The initial investment in the SOS program was $5.1 million annually. Program administrators were faced with the decision to either increase internal capacity by hiring more care coordinators and peers or to build a grant program. Rather than relying solely on internal care coordinators (which would have served an estimated 3,000 individuals annually), the team chose to fund community-based organizations. In just one year, 41 grantees reached more than 19,000 SMVF individuals, significantly exceeding projections for the number of veterans that would be served in the first year (see Figure 2-3). Infusing funding into the community was critical for taking the impact of the program to scale.

Grantee Diversity and Impact

Jancaitis reported that about half of the SOS grantees are clinical in nature with an outpatient counseling model and the other half are community-based efforts that provide a range of services including peer support, animal therapy, and case management. SOS grantees utilize a variety of evidence-based assessments (see Figure 2-4) to screen for behavioral health needs and suicide risk. After screening, SOS grantees directly provide support or refer those in need to other partner agencies for additional support.

In addition to the range in types of services offered, SOS grantees also range in size. This leads to some challenges with measurement, Jancaitis noted. One small standalone grantee might hire 1.5 people to provide services, while another grantee might be a larger organization with a 60-person team that pools SOS funds with Cohen Veterans Network[2] and Fox Grant Program funds, as well as private funding. She stated that the question of how to tell the story of program impacts in a way that a little "mom and pop" grantee does not get dwarfed and bigger grantees still shine as well is a challenge SOS program leaders grapple with daily.

---

[2] The Cohen Veterans Network (https://www.cohenveteransnetwork.org/) is a national non-profit organization that works to strengthen mental health outcomes, complement existing support, and improve quality of life for veterans and their families.

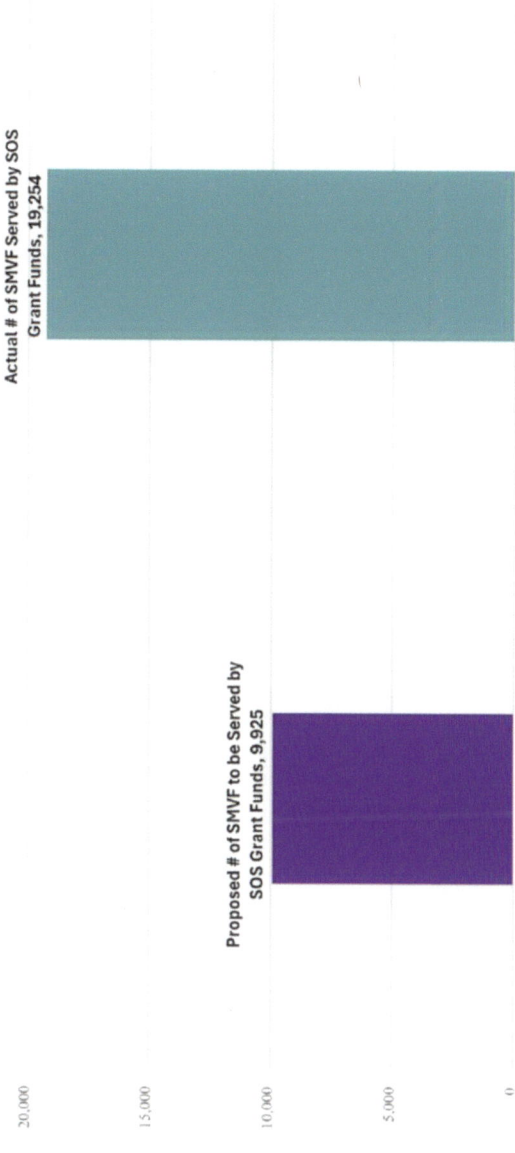

FIGURE 2-3 Virginia Department of Veterans Services Suicide Prevention and Opioid Addiction Services (SOS) Community Grant first year outcomes.
NOTE: SMVF = service members, veterans, and their families.
SOURCE: Presented by Brandi Jancaitis on April 29, 2025; Virginia Department of Veterans Services (2024, p. 89).

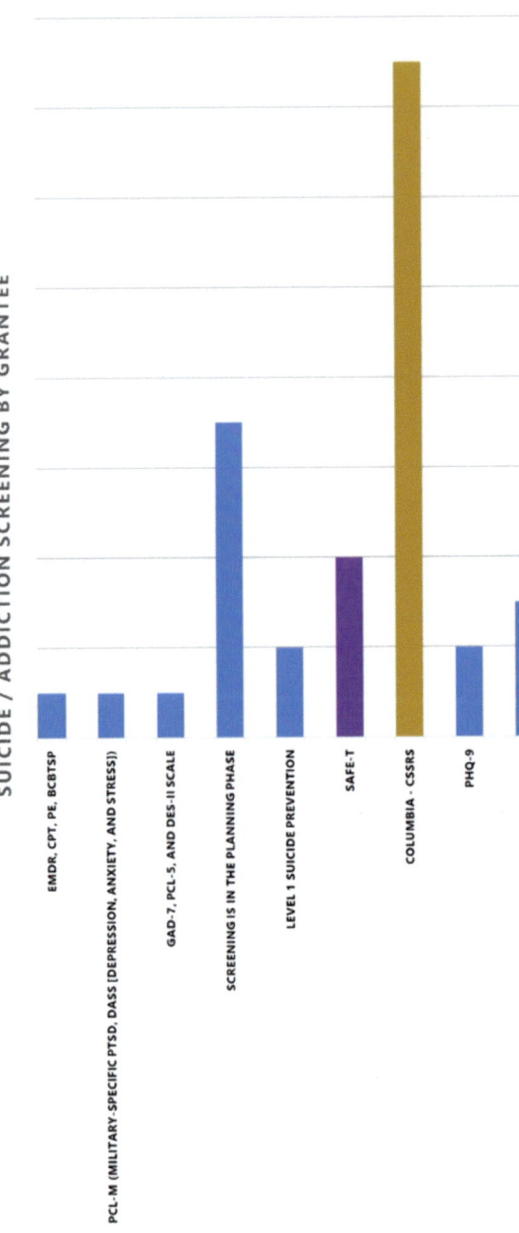

FIGURE 2-4 Screening tools used by Virginia Department of Veterans Services Suicide Prevention and Opioid Addiction Services (SOS) grantees.
NOTE: BCBTSP = Brief Cognitive-Behavioral Therapy for Suicide Prevention; CPT = Cognitive Processing Therapy; CSSRS = Columbia-Suicide Severity Rating Scale; DASS = Depression Anxiety Stress Scale; DES-II = Dissociative Experiences Scale; EMDR = Eye Movement Desensitization and Reprocessing therapy; GAD-7 = Generalized Anxiety Disorder-7; PCL-5 = PTSD Checklist for DSM-5; PCL-M = PTSD Checklist – Military Version; PE = Prolonged Exposure Therapy; PHQ-9 = Patient Health Questionnaire-9; PROMIS-29 = Patient-Reported Outcomes Measurement Information System-29; PTSD = Post-traumatic Stress Disorder; SAFE-T = Suicide Assessment Five Step Evaluation and Triage.
SOURCE: Presented by Brandi Jancaitis on April 29, 2025; Virginia Department of Veterans Services (2024, p. 90).

Employing military-connected individuals is another priority of the SOS program, Jancaitis shared. In addition to providing direct behavioral health and supportive services to individuals and families, SOS grantees hired over 70 military-connected individuals, contributing to Virginia Department of Veterans Services priority to support the entrepreneurial and career development goals of SMVF in local communities.

Jancaitis briefly highlighted the work of the eight SOS research grantees. SOS has both in-state and out-of-state partners working on topics such as adapting clinical best practices, surveying military-connected individuals to understand factors like disability status and military discharge implications and exploring a variety of risk and resilient factors among the military-connected population. She noted that one private research firm is examining the efficacy of community-based suicide prevention programs in Virginia.

Collaboration has been central to the SOS program's success, Jancaitis explained. The program team partners with the Virginia Department of Behavioral Health and 988 call centers. The SOS program is the key trainer for the 988 call specialists in Virginia, providing information on military culture and what SMVF resources are available in the state. The SOS program has leveraged work on lethal means safety education and awareness with Lock and Talk Virginia.[3] Jancaitis added that one of the umbrellas that has brought these partners together is the Governor's Challenge to Prevent Suicide.[4] Jancaitis concluded by underscoring the importance of this umbrella and the state investment in capacity for the success of the SOS program.

WHITE MOUNTAIN APACHE CELEBRATING LIFE SUICIDE PREVENTION PROGRAM

Mary Cwik and Novalene Alsenay Goklish (both with the Center for Indigenous Health, Bloomberg School of Public Health, Johns Hopkins University) described the White Mountain Apache Celebrating Life Suicide Prevention Program, which is a community-led, culturally grounded suicide prevention program developed in partnership with the Johns Hopkins University Center for Indigenous Health.

---

[3] Lock and Talk Virginia (https://www.lockandtalk.org/) is a statewide initiative that works to increase community engagement around mental health and advocate for the safe handling of lethal means like firearms and medications.

[4] The Governor's and Mayor's Challenges to Prevent Suicide Among Service Members, Veterans, and their Families (https://www.samhsa.gov/technical-assistance/smvf/challenges) are nationwide initiatives led by the Substance Abuse and Mental Health Services Administration (SAMHSA) and the VA to help states and communities implement comprehensive, coordinated suicide prevention strategies tailored to military-connected populations.

Tribal Context and Early Response to Suicide

Goklish, who is a member of the White Mountain Apache Tribe, described the context from the program. The White Mountain Apache Tribe resides on a 1.6-million-acre reservation (approximately the size of Delaware) in eastern Arizona with over 17,500 enrolled tribal members. Tribal members continue to practice traditional customs and language and are governed by an 11-member tribal council. She noted the tribe has partnered with Johns Hopkins University for over 40 years.

Goklish explained that suicide was rare in the community prior to the 1950s, and episodic spikes in youth suicide began to emerge in the 1990s. The tribe requested assistance from Johns Hopkins University in 1992 to understand and address suicide in the community. Suicide is taboo in Native American communities, Goklish shared, so it was difficult for community members to understand what was happening and how to address the problem.

Following another spike in suicide deaths in 2000, the tribe passed a resolution in 2002 mandating reporting of suicidal behaviors, including ideation, attempts, and deaths, as well as non-suicidal self-injury and binge substance use, and the tribe worked with Johns Hopkins University to set up the Celebrating Life Suicide Prevention Program, which includes surveillance of suicidal and other harmful behaviors and a case management system, Goklish reported.

The Celebrating Life Surveillance and Case Management System

Cwik highlighted impactful aspects of the Celebrating Life surveillance system, noting that the data are collected in real time, the community owns the data, and they know the data avoid the problem of racial and ethnic misidentification that can come with larger data-gathering efforts. The data enable them to look at risk and protective factors and patterns in suicide over time to understand the impacts the program is making in their communities.

Goklish noted that in 2006, the tribal resolution was expanded to require reservation-wide reporting from all community members and first responders, and to ensure that referrals were being sent to the Celebrating Life program. Goklish described efforts undertaken by trained case managers under the program. They conduct in-person follow-ups for each report of suicidal behavior or substance use, verify incident details, provide wellness checks, assist with referrals, and engage in problem-solving related to accessing services. Case managers work with the individual to identify solutions to problems they are facing and how to address circumstances that may lead them to feel that they do not have a lot that is positive happening in their lives. Goklish added examples of the types of challenges that case managers may help individuals overcome, such as wanting to return to school or to find housing.

Goklish listed the three culturally adapted components of the Celebrating Life program designed to complement the surveillance and case management system:

- Elders Resilience Curriculum,
- New Hope risk reduction intervention, and
- Bright Horizons substance abuse prevention and intervention.

She provided a brief overview of the Elders' Resilience Curriculum, a school-based program that delivers monthly lessons to students in grades 3 through 8. The program focuses on suicide prevention, but the Elders do not speak directly about suicide. Rather, the Elders discuss topics such as respect, Apache culture, endurance, self-worth, and communication. The program reflects the community's view that teaching Apache culture and speaking the language is an important way to build connectedness, identity, and strength.

Cwik explained that the Celebrating Life program takes a comprehensive public health approach to suicide prevention as there is no single intervention that will lead to zero suicide. She turned to describing the New Hope component of the program, which is a brief, community-delivered intervention designed for individuals at high risk following an acute suicide event such as suicidal ideation or an attempt leading to an emergency room visit. Delivered by trained Apache paraprofessionals, the intervention includes safety planning and addresses barriers to accessing mental health care. It is designed to be delivered in one or two sessions totaling only two to four hours because lengthier treatment programs may not be realistic in some community contexts.

Celebrating Life Program Impact

Celebrating Life has been associated with substantial reductions in suicide outcomes, Cwik shared. During a five-year period when multiple community-based interventions were active, the tribe saw a 38 percent reduction in suicide deaths and a 53 percent reduction in suicide attempts (see Figure 2-5). These findings contributed to the program receiving funding from the National Institutes of Health to formally evaluate New Hope and the Elders' Resilience Curriculum through a study involving over 300 Apache youth and young adults aged 10–29; findings from the evaluation will be published soon.

Goklish noted that inequities in suicide death rates in American Indian and Alaska Native youth are expected to continue to widen unless

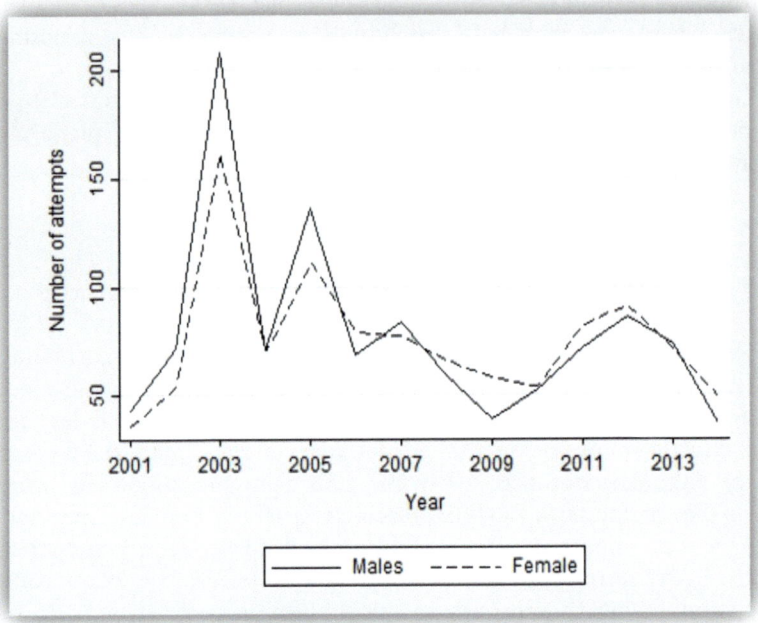
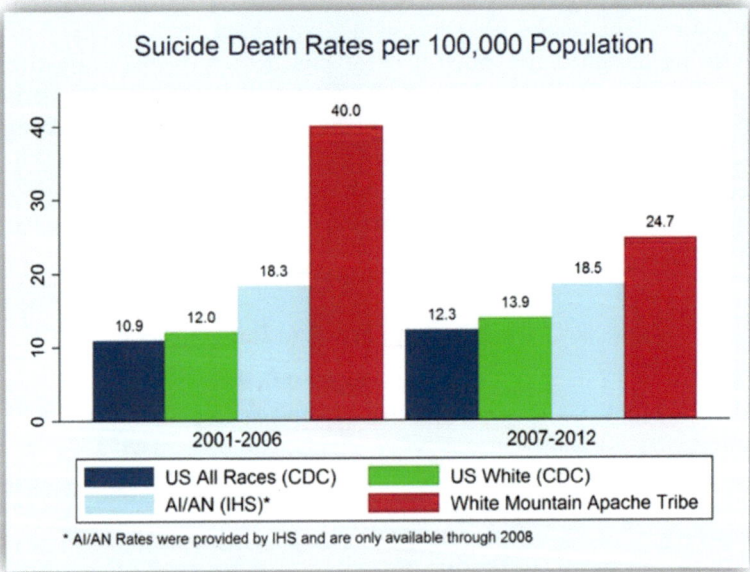

FIGURE 2-5 Suicide attempts and deaths among the White Mountain Apache Tribe.
SOURCE: Presented by Mary Cwik and Novalene Alsenay Goklish on April 29, 2025.

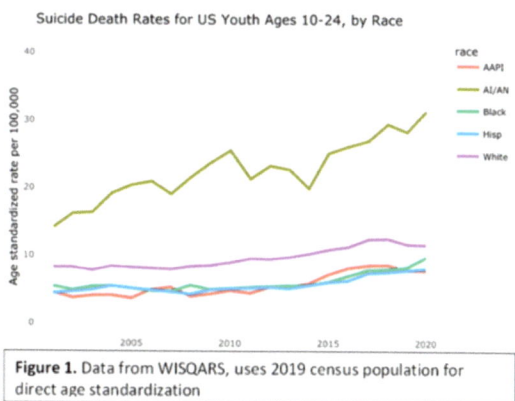

FIGURE 2-6 Suicide death rates for U.S. youth ages 10–24, by race.
SOURCE: Presented by Mary Cwik and Novalene Alsenay Goklish on April 29, 2025.

interventions are scaled (see Figure 2-6). Cwik added that other tribal communities have shown interest in the Celebrating Life approach, and Johns Hopkins has provided technical assistance to tribes including the Navajo Nation, San Carlos Apache, Hualapai, and Cherokee Nation in adapting the surveillance and case management system.

Cwik concluded by highlighting the importance of tribal sovereignty in enabling innovative, collective responses to suicide prevention. The White Mountain Apache model demonstrates that communities benefit from combining crisis response with upstream, preventive strategies that are culturally relevant and locally managed. She emphasized that Indigenous and veteran communities are both at the forefront of suicide prevention, with valuable insights to offer the broader field.

GARRETT LEE SMITH AND NATIVE CONNECTIONS SUICIDE PREVENTION PROGRAMS

Richard McKeon (Senior Advisor, SAMHSA) discussed the Garrett Lee Smith (GLS) and Native Connections suicide prevention programs administered by SAMHSA. He began by noting that community-based suicide prevention is the first strategic direction in the revised U.S. National Strategy for Suicide Prevention.[5]

---

[5] https://www.hhs.gov/programs/prevention-and-wellness/mental-health-substance-use-disorder/national-strategy-suicide-prevention/index.html

Origin and Structure of the GLS Program

The GLS suicide prevention program was established through the Garrett Lee Smith Memorial Act, which was passed in 2004 following the death by suicide of Garrett Lee Smith, son of U.S. Senator Gordon Smith, McKeon explained. Senator Smith considered resigning from the Senate in the wake of this tragedy, but realized he could do more to honor his son's memory by working to advance youth suicide prevention efforts at the federal level.

McKeon stated that the GLS program includes three components:

- State and Tribal Youth Suicide Prevention Grants
- Campus Suicide Prevention Grants
- Suicide Prevention Resource Center

Table 2-1 presents a comparison of the grant-making components of the GLS program. McKeon focused on the State and Tribal Youth Suicide Prevention Grants for the GLS component of his presentation.

In contrast to the Staff Sargeant Parker Gordon Fox Suicide Prevention Grant Program, McKeon noted, GLS State and Tribal Youth Suicide Prevention Grants are awarded to state agencies or tribes, rather than individual organizations, though those entities may designate an organization to administer the funds. For example, the White Mountain Apache Tribe designated Johns Hopkins Center for Indigenous Health and the state of New Hampshire designated National Alliance on Mental Illness New Hampshire. The state and tribal grants require that recipients implement activities as part of a comprehensive youth suicide prevention plan. The program focuses on youth and young adults, historically ages 10–24, though SAMHSA recently removed the lower age limit to support earlier interventions.

TABLE 2-1 Comparison of the Grant-Making Components of the Garrett Lee Smith (GLS) Program

GLS State/Tribal	GLS Campus
5-year grant	3-year grant
Available to states and tribes	Available to higher education institutions
Supports suicide prevention activities, through a public health approach, for youth up to 24 years old	Supports student suicide prevention activities
$735,000/year	$102,000/year (requires matching funds)

SOURCE: Staff generated based on presentation by Richard McKeon on April 29, 2025.

McKeon reported that GLS-funded activities include screening and gatekeeper training (e.g., Question, Persuade, and Refer [commonly referred to as QPR], Alcohol, Smoking and Substance Involvement Screening Test [commonly referred to as ASSIST]), improving care transitions, follow-up after emergency room discharge, use of hotlines (now promoting 988), enhancing social connectedness, engaging high-risk populations such as youth in foster care or engaged with the juvenile justice system, and improving lethal means safety.

Evaluation Findings, Impact, and Program Reach

McKeon shared that the initial thinking was that providing a three-year grant and then having grantees develop a sustainability program would be sufficient, but evaluation findings demonstrated sustained investment yields stronger outcomes. Initial evaluations showed reductions in youth suicide after one year of GLS programming. However, impacts declined once programming stopped, prompting SAMHSA to lengthen and increase grant funding. As shown in Figure 2-7, more recent evaluations using propensity score matching[6] showed that counties with four consecutive years of GLS programming experienced greater reductions in youth suicide than counties with shorter durations of programming. GLS results show that suicide prevention is never a one-and-done effort and underscore the importance of ongoing funding to support community-based efforts for sustaining significant impacts, McKeon added.

McKeon turned to discussing the geographic reach of the GLS program. As shown in Figure 2-8, in fiscal year (FY) 2021, GLS State and Tribal Grants were awarded to 24 states, 2 U.S. territories, and 28 tribes. While the program had national reach, it did not touch every county, which allowed for comparison in evaluations.

Native Connections Program

McKeon concluded his presentation with a brief description of SAMHSA's Native Connections (Tribal Behavioral Health) program, which was developed to offer a grant-based structure specifically for tribal suicide prevention. Unlike GLS, which was competitive and focused on youth, Native Connections began with the idea of universal tribal grants modeled after state

---

[6] Propensity score matching is a statistical technique used to pair individuals in a treatment or intervention group with individuals in a control group based on similar propensity scores (the estimated probability of receiving the treatment given their observed baseline characteristics). This approach creates matched pairs that are similar on key factors (such as age, health status, or income), helping to ensure that any observed differences in outcomes are more likely attributable to the treatment itself rather than to underlying differences between the groups.

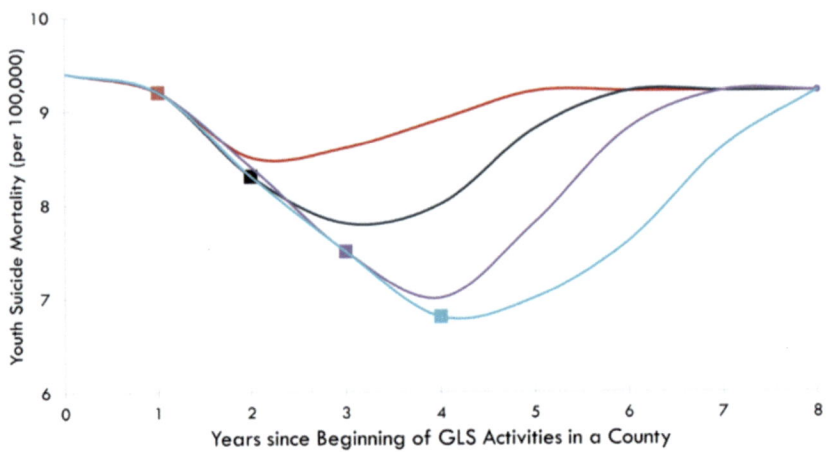

FIGURE 2-7 Impact of Garrett Lee Smith (GLS) programming by duration of exposure.
SOURCE: Presented by Richard McKeon on April 29, 2025; U.S. Department of Health and Human Services (2024a, p. 46).

block grants. Although the formula-based model was not adopted, competitive grants were launched, with Congress directing SAMHSA to target tribes with high suicide rates—though McKeon noted that tribal-specific suicide data were not available at the time. SAMHSA staff worked with tribes to help them calculate their rate using CDC data and determine whether they were above the midpoint for American Indian and Alaska Native suicide rates nationally. Each Native Connections grant is $250,000 annually.

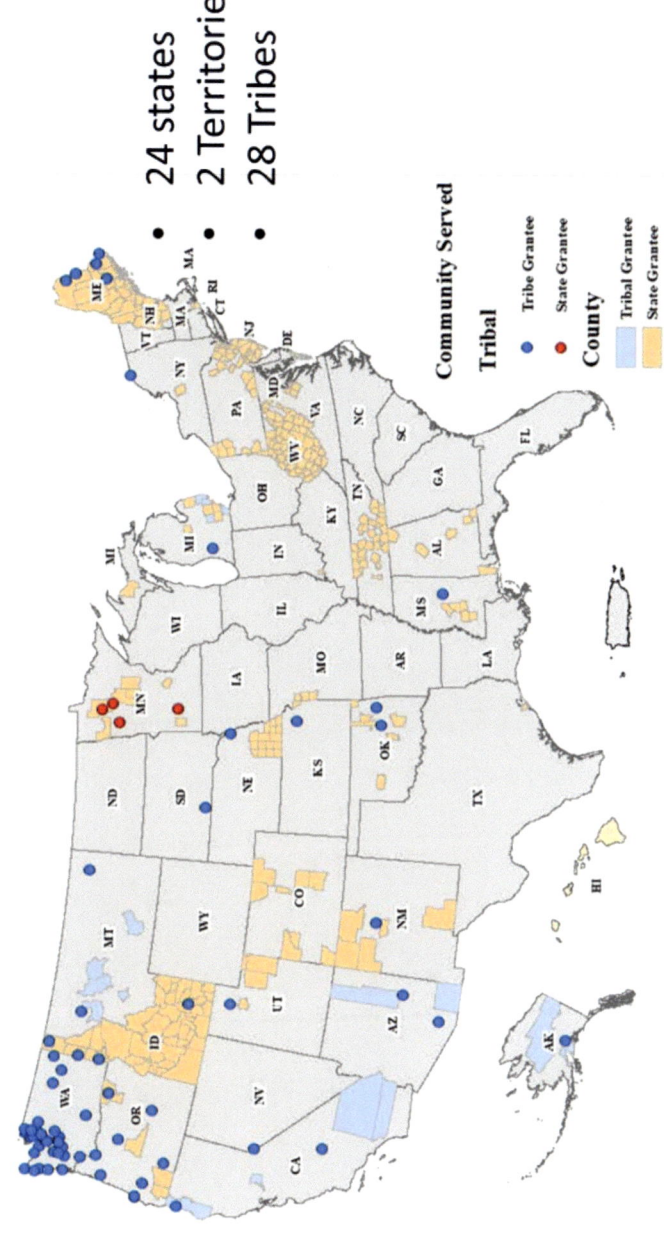

FIGURE 2-8 Map of Garrett Lee Smith (GLS) state and tribal grantees, FY 2021.
SOURCE: Presented by Richard McKeon on April 29, 2025.

REFERENCES

Bryan, C. J., & Rudd, M. D. (2018). *Brief cognitive-behavioral therapy for suicide prevention*. The Guilford Press.

Posner, K., Brown, G. K., Stanley, B., Brent, D. A., Yershova, K. V., Oquendo, M. A., Currier, G. W., Melvin, G. A., Greenhill, L., Shen, S., & Mann, J. J. (2011). The Columbia-Suicide Severity Rating Scale: Initial validity and internal consistency findings from three multisite studies with adolescents and adults. *American Journal of Psychiatry, 168*(12), 1266–1277. https://doi.org/10.1176/appi.ajp.2011.10111704

U.S. Department of Veterans Affairs. (2024a). *National strategy for suicide prevention*. https://www.hhs.gov/sites/default/files/national-strategy-suicide-prevention.pdf

___. (2024b). *2024 national veteran suicide prevention annual report. Part 1 of 2: In-depth reviews*. https://www.mentalhealth.va.gov/docs/data-sheets/2024/2024-Annual-Report-Part-1-of-2_508.pdf

Virginia Department of Veterans Services (2024, December 1). *Commissioner's 2024 annual report to Governor Glenn Youngkin, Secretary Craig Crenshaw, and the Virginia General Assembly*. https://rga.lis.virginia.gov/Published/2024/RD907/PDF

3

Considerations for Program Development and Oversight and Grantee-Level Implementation and Performance Metrics

Building on the program examples presented in the preceding session, the next workshop session focused on considerations for program development and oversight, as well as grantee-level implementation and performance metrics. These closely connected topics were addressed together in a single session to foster cohesive dialogue on design, delivery, and oversight. The session opened with a series of brief presentations that provided a foundation for two moderated panel discussions. The first panel discussion focused on lessons learned from the programs described in the previous session. In the second panel discussion, other invited experts offered perspectives on questions related to program development, oversight, and implementation. The session concluded with a round of audience Q&A.

With emphasis on the public health approach, this chapter presents practical strategies for designing and overseeing non-clinical suicide prevention programs implemented at the community level. Drawing on foundational presentations and two panel discussions, participants explored how programs can be tailored to local capacity, needs, and cultural context; supported through proactive technical assistance; and evaluated using realistic metrics that reflect incremental progress. Additional topics included the development of theories of change and logic models, the use of dashboards and storytelling to communicate impact, equitable funding structures, and approaches to cultivating strong grantee networks and clarifying inclusion criteria.

FOUNDATIONAL PRESENTATIONS

Foundational presentations covered a range of topics. Following an introductory talk, presenters addressed the public health approach to comprehensive suicide prevention, models for effective community-based programs, the development of logic models, strategies for providing comprehensive technical assistance, and the use of data dashboards to support program implementation and oversight.

Theory of Change, Theory of Action, and Performance Metrics

Daniel Friend (Mathematica; member, workshop planning committee) kicked off the session with a presentation assembled in collaboration with Elly Stout (Education Development Center [EDC]; member, workshop planning committee). Friend opened by highlighting the importance of grounding programs in a cohesive theory of change and identifying realistic performance metrics. He noted that context is key, and it is important to consider who is being served by a program. A cohesive theory of change links program activities to their intended outcomes. Friend explained that the structure begins with activities—the mechanisms through which change is introduced—and then flows through a logical sequence of outcome stages:

- Change outcomes refer to proximal effects, such as shifts in attitudes, knowledge, or skills.
- Short- and intermediate-term outcomes reflect more distal changes, such as sustained use of knowledge and skills.
- Long-term outcomes represent broader population health improvements.

Friend used a psychoeducational workshop focused on resilience-building as an illustrative example of a cohesive theory of change (see Figure 3-1). A successful activity of this kind might reduce stigmatizing attitudes and improve social support (change outcomes), which in turn could increase help-seeking behaviors (intermediate outcome), ultimately contributing to a reduction in suicidal behaviors (long-term outcome).

Friend emphasized the distinction between a theory of change (which explains how change is achieved) and a theory of action (which ensures implementation quality). The latter is supported by performance metrics—quantitative indicators that track progress toward a particular target and guide decision-making (see Figure 3-2). Friend stressed that metrics are a cornerstone of continuous quality improvement. For instance, if a program has a goal of recruiting 100 veterans per month but is only enrolling 12, this indicates a need for strategic adjustment, such as changing

CONSIDERATIONS FOR PROGRAM DEVELOPMENT AND OVERSIGHT 29

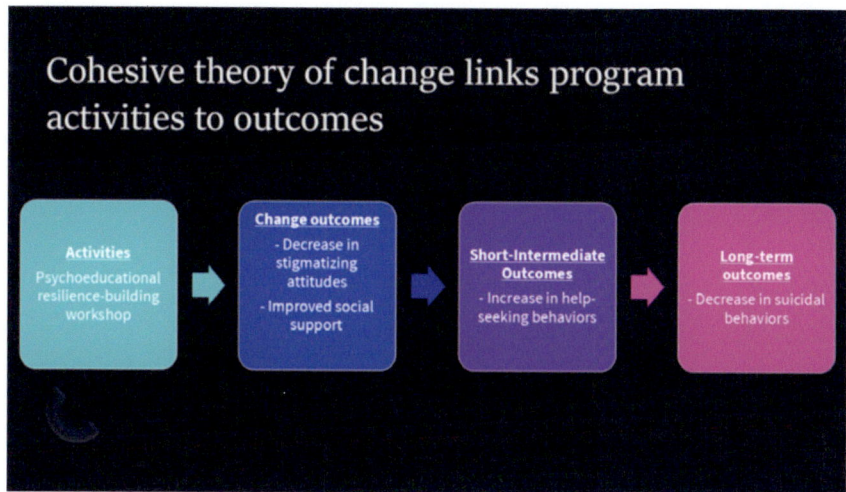

FIGURE 3-1 Psychoeducational resilience-building workshop as an illustrative example of a cohesive theory of change.
SOURCE: Presented by Daniel Friend on April 29, 2025.

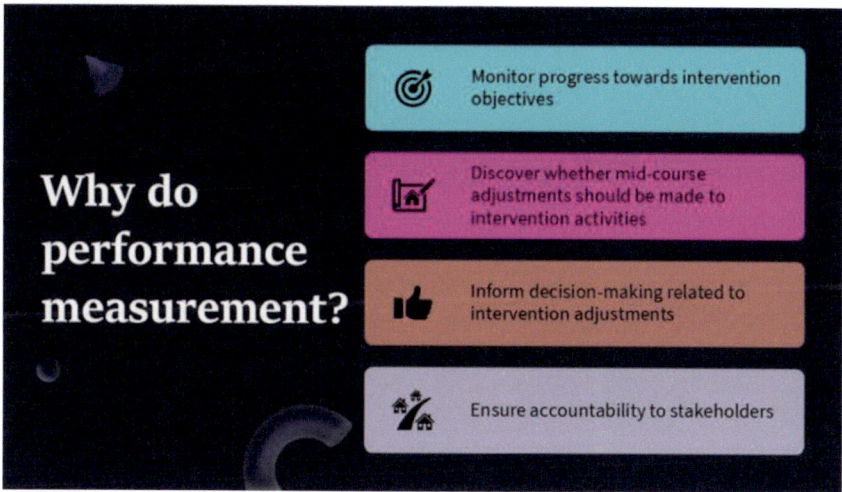

FIGURE 3-2 Why do performance measurement?
SOURCE: Presented by Daniel Friend on April 29, 2025.

recruitment strategies. Realistic and achievable metrics allow for responsive management and improvement and help to ensure accountability to various stakeholders.

Drawing from experience across programs, Friend identified several common performance metrics that can be adapted based on program context:

- Recruitment and enrollment
- Dose (extent of services received)
- Initial engagement
- Service uptake
- Satisfaction and acceptability to participants
- Fidelity (adherence to the program model)
- Feasibility
- Sustainability
- Cost

Together, all of these metrics not only help ensure accountability but also serve as key inputs into program implementation as well as guiding program evaluation, Friend concluded.

The Public Health Approach and Comprehensive Suicide Prevention

Alex Crosby (Morehouse School of Medicine) provided an in-depth presentation on the public health approach to comprehensive suicide prevention, emphasizing its systematic methodology and application to reducing suicidal behaviors across diverse populations.

Crosby began by introducing the public health framework, noting its four core components: assessing the problem, identifying causes, developing and testing interventions, and disseminating and implementing successful strategies (see Figure 3-3). This structured method allows public health practitioners to systematically understand suicide-related issues and effectively intervene across different community contexts.

Assessing the problem involves developing understanding of the scope and nature of suicide by examining who is affected, where incidents occur, and the broader circumstances surrounding suicidal behaviors, Crosby explained. Identifying causes involves examining "why" questions, such as why suicide might be more prevalent in one population than another—e.g., urban versus rural, males versus females. After gaining understanding around aspects of the "why," the next step is developing and testing programs and policies tailored to address these factors. Crosby offered as an example developing an intervention to reduce alcohol misuse because substance misuse, particularly alcohol misuse, is a major risk factor for

- The public health approach seeks to answer the foundational questions:
  - What is the problem?
  - How could we prevent it from occurring?
- To answer these questions, public health uses a systematic, scientific method for understanding and preventing suicide.

FIGURE 3-3 Public health approach to suicide prevention.
SOURCE: Presentation by Alex Crosby on April 29, 2025; based on discussion in Potter and colleagues (1995) and World Health Organization (2014).

suicidal behavior. The final step in the public health approach entails expanding the reach of successful programs and disseminating lessons from such programs.

Crosby highlighted historical trends, noting suicide rates in the United States dating back to the 1930s. He pointed out that during the 1920s and 1930s, the Great Depression significantly influenced higher suicide rates, demonstrating the critical impact of economic factors on suicidal behaviors. Crosby stressed the importance of recognizing the multifaceted nature of suicide, cautioning against attributing rising suicide rates to any single factor, but rather understanding it as resulting from complex interactions of multiple determinants.

Examining recent trends, Crosby presented data showing increased suicide rates across various demographic groups, including age, sex, and racial/ethnic categories. Between 1999 and 2023, suicide rates notably increased across almost all age groups for both males and females, except for males aged 75 and older, where rates remained relatively stable (see Figure 3-4). Similarly, data disaggregated by race and ethnicity indicated increasing suicide rates among White, Hispanic, Black, and Asian American populations, and particularly high increases among American Indian and Alaska Native populations. Crosby emphasized this widespread increase to underline the need for broad-based suicide prevention efforts (see Figure 3-5).

Crosby also highlighted suicide rates among veterans (see Figure 3-6) compared to non-veterans, revealing ongoing challenges despite slight

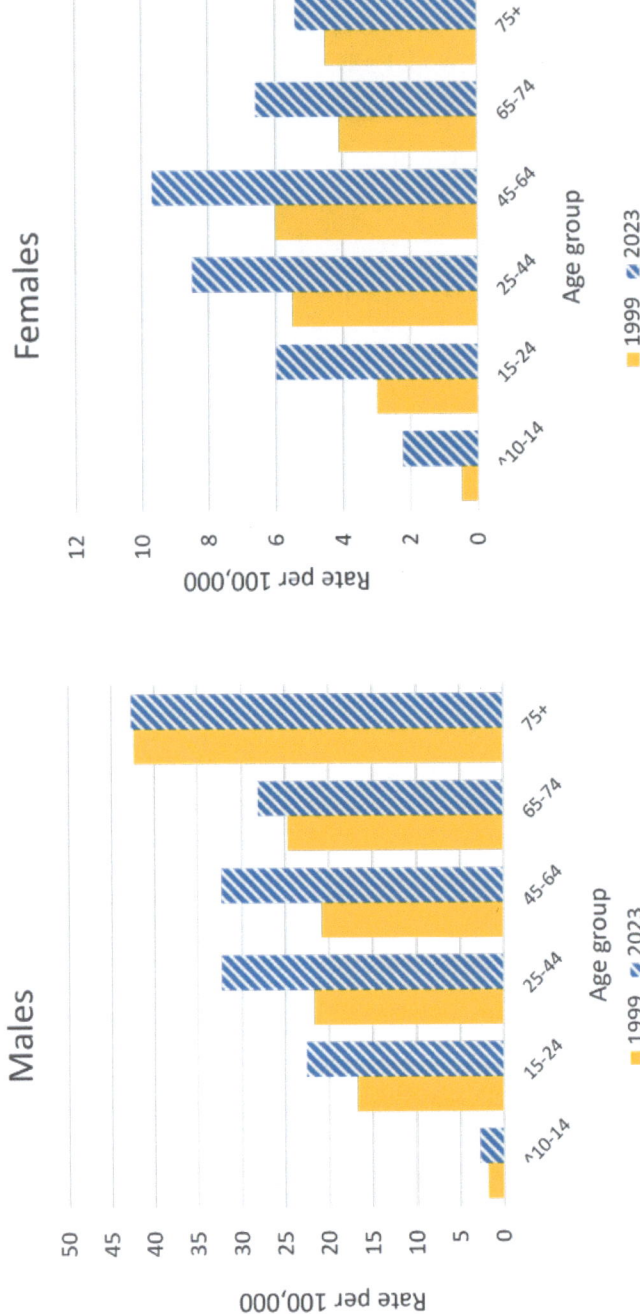

FIGURE 3-4 Suicide rates by age group and sex, 1999 versus 2023.
SOURCE: Hedegaard and colleagues (2020). Presentation by Alex Crosby on April 29, 2025.

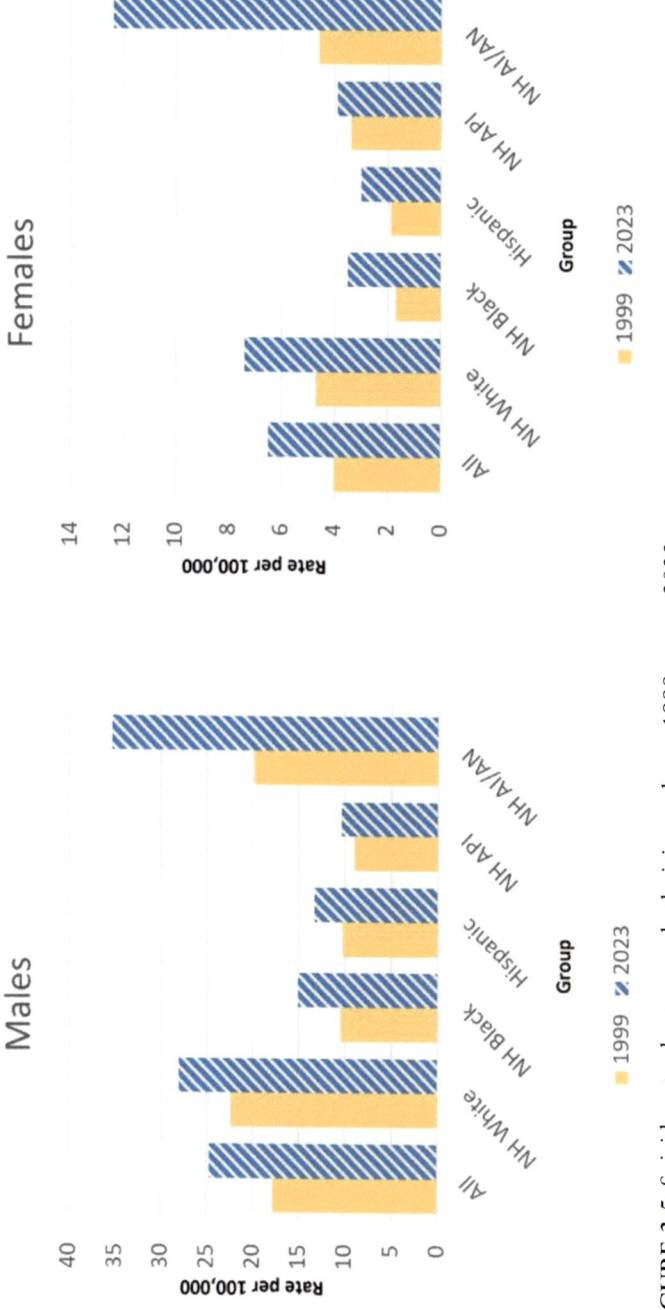

FIGURE 3-5 Suicide rates by race and ethnicity and sex, 1999 versus 2023.
SOURCES: Presentation by Alex Crosby on April 29, 2025; based on data from CDC Web-Based Injury Statistics Query and Reporting System (WISQARS, https://www.cdc.gov/injury/wisqars/index.html) and Curtin and Hedegaard (2019).

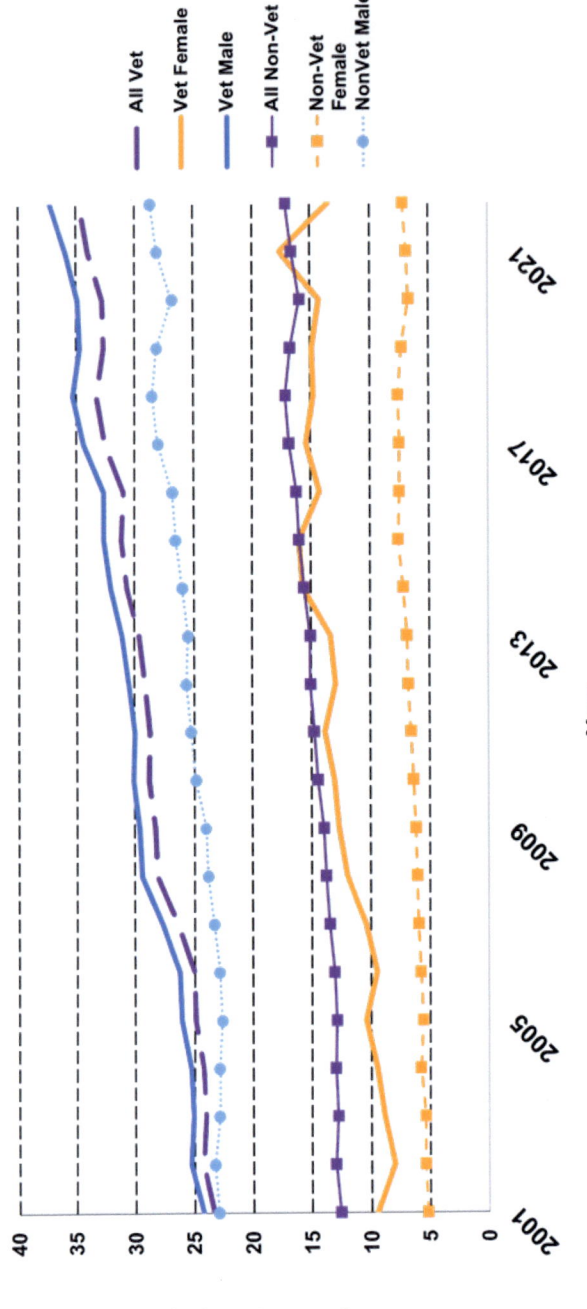

FIGURE 3-6 Veteran and non-veteran suicide rates, 2001 to 2022.
SOURCE: Presentation by Alex Crosby on April 29, 2025; based on data in U.S. Department of Veterans Affairs (2024).

improvements in recent years. This underscored the importance of targeted suicide prevention strategies tailored specifically to the veteran community.

Crosby explained that it is important to consider the impacts of suicidal behaviors beyond mortality. Suicide-related hospitalizations, emergency department visits, reported attempts, and serious ideation occur with progressively greater frequency. While approximately 46,000 suicides occurred in 2021, millions more experienced serious suicidal ideation or attempts, representing critical intervention opportunities to prevent suicides, Crosby noted (see Figure 3-7). He added that those at risk of suicide are often dealing with multiple issues that can be at the individual level, at the family or peer level, at the community level, or at the societal level. For example, an individual might be facing housing insecurity, chronic illness, and hunger or food insecurity simultaneously. Intervening on just one of these issues might be enough to decrease their risk for suicidal behavior, Crosby suggested.

Crosby outlined the Centers for Disease Control and Prevention's (CDC's) Comprehensive Suicide Prevention program, describing key components such as strong leadership, multisectoral partnerships, and the use

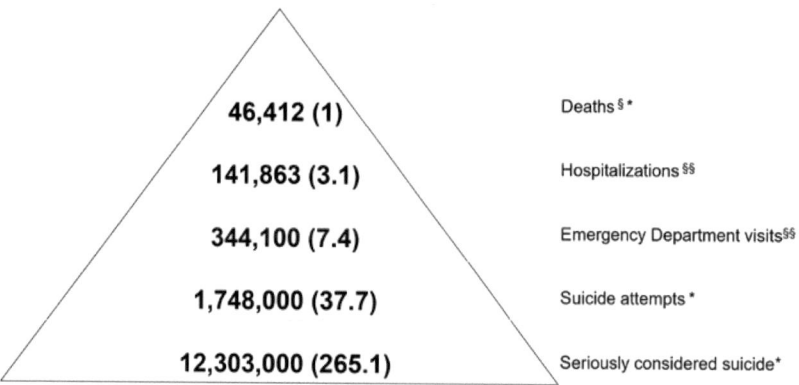

FIGURE 3-7 Scope of suicide-related thoughts and behaviors among U.S. adults, 2021.
NOTE: Numbers in parentheses indicate the ratio of each category relative to suicide deaths.
§ Centers for Disease Control and Prevention's (CDC's) National Vital Statistics System (https://www.cdc.gov/nchs/nvss/index.htm).
§§ CDC's National Electronic Injury Surveillance System-All Injury Program (https://www.cpsc.gov/Research--Statistics/NEISS-Injury-Data).
* Substance Abuse and Mental Health Services Administration's National Survey on Drug Use and Health (https://www.samhsa.gov/data/data-we-collect/nsduh-national-survey-drug-use-and-health).
SOURCE: Presentation by Alex Crosby on April 29, 2025; Crosby and colleagues (2011).

of data-driven strategies. He discussed CDC's approach to identifying disproportionately affected populations—populations that experience rates of suicide greater than the general population, which include veterans, tribal populations, rural communities, LGBTQ+ individuals, and youth.

To illustrate comprehensive suicide prevention strategies, Crosby described CDC's *Suicide Prevention Resource for Action*, which identifies specific strategies and approaches supported by evidence (see Table 3-1). Crosby pointed out evidence indicating that communities implementing multiple strategies simultaneously experienced greater success compared to those employing single-strategy interventions.

In describing upstream suicide prevention, Crosby referred to the visual metaphor illustrated in Figure 3-8. He likened suicide risk to individuals falling through a gap in a bridge into a river leading to a waterfall downstream, describing different points along the river where interventions might occur. As shown in the figure, the furthest upstream strategy is to repair the gap in the bridge, an approach Crosby equated with strategies such as strengthening economic supports and building coping and problem-solving skills. Midstream interventions might focus on reducing substance misuse, while crisis response is often necessary downstream. Crosby emphasized that public health approaches, including those discussed throughout the workshop, address all of these levels simultaneously. However, he stressed that upstream strategies tend to be the most effective and cost-efficient. Even so, midstream and downstream interventions remain vital, as not everyone can be reached early.

TABLE 3-1 Comprehensive Suicide Prevention Strategies and Approaches

Strategy	Approach
Strengthen economic supports	Household financial security, housing stabilization policies
Create protective environments	Reducing access to lethal means, organizational policies, community-based alcohol reduction policies
Strengthen access and delivery of suicide care	Mental health coverage, reduce provider shortages in underserved areas, safer suicide care through systems change
Promote healthy connections	Peer norm programs, community engagement activities
Teach coping and problem-solving skills	Social-emotional learning programs, parenting skills and family relationship approaches
Identify and support people at risk	Gatekeeper training, crisis intervention, treatment for at-risk individuals, prevention of re-attempts
Lessen harms and prevent future risk	Postvention activities, safe reporting and messaging about suicide

SOURCE: Presentation by Alex Crosby on April 29, 2025; Centers for Disease Control and Prevention (2022).

- Cognitive behavioral
- Crisis response

- Gatekeeper training
- Reduce Substance misuse

- Economic supports
- Coping or problem-solving skills

FIGURE 3-8 Illustrative model for suicide prevention across the continuum of risk.
SOURCE: Presentation by Alex Crosby on April 29, 2025; Wisconsin Department of Health Services (n.d., p. 1), reprinted with permission.

Concluding his presentation, Crosby reiterated that suicidality is a critical, multifaceted public health issue. He stressed the necessity of a comprehensive, evidence-informed approach, emphasizing that effectively addressing suicide requires interventions at multiple levels—individual, family, community, and societal. Crosby affirmed that tailored strategies responsive to specific community needs and protective factors are essential for meaningful reductions in suicidal behaviors.

Models for Effective Community Suicide Prevention

Stout presented an overview of models and tools that can support the design and implementation of effective community-based suicide prevention efforts. She emphasized the importance of helping communities adapt concepts and strategies to fit their specific needs, assets, and levels of readiness.

Stout opened by noting that community suicide prevention has long been a priority in national strategies, including the 2012 National Strategy for Suicide Prevention and more recent updates. While national strategies outline broad goals and objectives, Stout explained, relatively few models are available that translate those goals into actionable guidance for communities. She highlighted three frameworks that offer communities clear direction on both what to implement and how to implement it.

The first framework Stout mentioned was the CDC Suicide Prevention Resource for Action, which outlines evidence-informed strategies for reducing suicide risk. As described earlier in Crosby's presentation on the public health approach and comprehensive suicide prevention, this resource identifies multiple areas for intervention that, when combined, are associated with greater impact (see Table 3-1). Stout clarified that CDC's resource focuses on broad strategies—such as strengthening economic supports or creating protective environments—rather than prescribing specific programs. The goal, she said, is to help communities prioritize and combine strategies based on their own context.

Stout next discussed the Suicide Prevention Resource Center's (SPRC's) Comprehensive Approach to Suicide Prevention,[1] which predates the CDC model but includes many of the same elements (see Figure 3-9). She described the visual representation of the model as a puzzle, with interconnected components that collectively support a comprehensive approach. Importantly, she noted that this is not a checklist; communities are not expected to implement every element. Rather, the model can help community stakeholders identify where they are currently investing and where additional focus may be needed.

To complement the SPRC framework, Stout introduced SPRC's Strategic Planning Approach, which offers a step-by-step process for tailoring community suicide prevention strategies (see Figure 3-10). The process includes assessing suicide-related risk and protective factors in the local community, identifying populations at highest risk, and taking stock of the local context, including assets and opportunities. From there, community leaders can select appropriate strategies from the CDC or SPRC models and identify culturally appropriate programs or practices for implementation. Evaluation is the final step in the cycle, allowing communities to assess whether they are making measurable progress toward reducing suicidal behaviors.

Stout then turned to a third model—EDC's Community-Led Suicide Prevention approach—which builds on the CDC and SPRC frameworks and incorporates insights from a 2017 National Action Alliance for Suicide Prevention report on transforming communities. That report reviewed global examples of community-based suicide prevention efforts and identified seven key elements that contribute to success (National Action Alliance for Suicide Prevention, 2017):

1. Unity
2. Strategic planning

---

[1] SPRC (https://sprc.org/) is a SAMHSA-funded resource center focused on advancing the implementation of the U.S. National Strategy for Suicide Prevention (https://www.hhs.gov/sites/default/files/national-strategy-suicide-prevention.pdf).

FIGURE 3-9 *What* to implement for effective community suicide prevention: Suicide Prevention Resource Center (SPRC) comprehensive approach.
SOURCE: Presentation by Elly Stout on April 29, 2025; SPRC (2020a). Developed by Education Development Center (EDC) at the University of Oklahoma under a cooperative agreement funded by the U.S. Department of Health and Human Services. Copyright © 2020 by the Board of Regents of the University of Oklahoma.

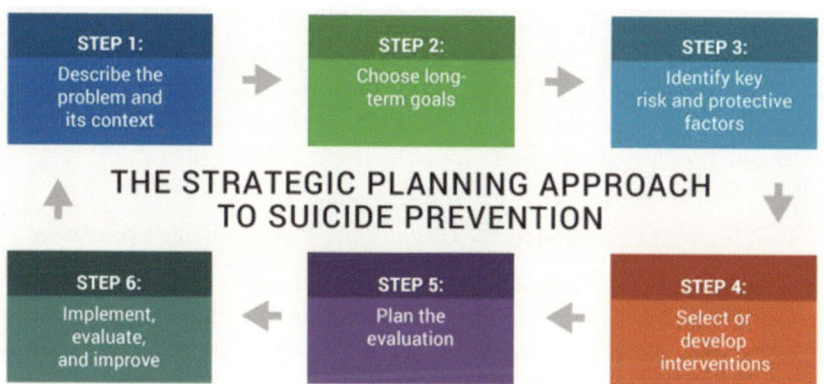

FIGURE 3-10 *How* to do effective community suicide prevention: Suicide Prevention Resource Center (SPRC) strategic planning approach.
SOURCE: Presentation by Elly Stout on April 29, 2025; SPRC (2020b). Developed by Education Development Center (EDC) at the University of Oklahoma under a cooperative agreement funded by the U.S. Department of Health and Human Services. Copyright © 2020 by the Board of Regents of the University of Oklahoma.

3. Integration
4. Sustainability
5. Data
6. Fit
7. Communication

Stout highlighted two of these components due to their relevance to discussions at this workshop. She explained that the unity component involves bringing community partners together and building consensus. With regard to the data component, she noted that it involved considering the local context and pointed to the White Mountain Apache surveillance system discussed earlier in the workshop (see Chapter 2) as an example of a culturally appropriate data system that also supports sustainability and effective communication.

Stout concluded by underscoring the value of grounding grant programs and community initiatives in structured, evidence-informed models. Doing so, she said, helps ensure that strategies are aligned with community needs and priorities, and gives communities a way to assess whether they are making progress toward meaningful outcomes. She encouraged participants to explore publicly available resources from CDC (Centers for Disease Control and Prevention, 2022), EDC (Education Development Center, 2025), the National Action Alliance for Suicide Prevention (2017), SPRC (2020a,b), U.S. Department of Health and Human Services (2024), and U.S. Department of Veterans Affairs (2018).

Developing Logic Models for Community-Based Suicide Prevention

Corbin Standley (American Foundation for Suicide Prevention [AFSP][2]) presented an overview of logic models and their role in guiding evaluation of community-based interventions. He described logic models as visual roadmaps that explain the relationship between a program's activities and its intended outcomes, provide a framework for both implementation and evaluation and making explicit the program's underlying logic. He added that logic models are typically one-page, iterative documents that evolve as programs mature and data become available.

Standley explained that logic models often include five core components:

---

[2] AFSP (https://afsp.org/) is a voluntary health organization dedicated to saving lives and bringing hope to those affected by suicide, including those who have experienced a loss. AFSP creates a culture that's smart about mental health through public education and community programs, develops suicide prevention through research and advocacy, and provides support for those affected by suicide.

CONSIDERATIONS FOR PROGRAM DEVELOPMENT AND OVERSIGHT 41

1. Goals, which define the overarching purpose of the program;
2. Learning objectives and program objectives;
3. Processes and activities carried out as part of the program;
4. Outcomes, including short-term and long-term changes; and
5. Context, which accounts for cultural and community considerations.

He underscored the importance of cultural humility and cultural appropriateness, working with the community to define problems needing to be addressed along with desired solutions.

To help orient the audience to terminology, Standley introduced a general template showing the relationship between inputs, activities, outputs, outcomes, and long-term impacts (see Figure 3-11). The framework shows how inputs such as funding, personnel, and materials support activities like training or outreach, which lead to outputs (e.g., number of presentations or attendees) and short-term outcomes—measurable changes you anticipate immediately following a program or intervention, such as knowledge gain or skill development. These, in turn, contribute to longer-term outcomes like reduced stigma, increased help-seeking behavior, and ultimately reduced suicide rates.

Standley then walked through a more detailed breakdown of each logic model component, offering specific guiding questions and prompts for program planners (see Figure 3-12A). For example, when defining inputs, program planners might ask what materials, training, and technology are needed. To illustrate how these principles are applied in practice, Standley shared a logic model used by the AFSP for its flagship education program, Talk Saves Lives (see Figure 3-12B). Inputs for the program include a scripted PowerPoint, an implementation guide, and evaluation tools. Activities include training volunteer presenters and delivering presentations in communities. Outputs track the number of trainings, attendees, and participant satisfaction. Short-term outcomes include increased knowledge of suicide prevention, improved attitudes and beliefs, greater self-efficacy, and reduced barriers to talking about suicide. While long-term impacts such as reduced suicide rates are more difficult to measure directly, they remain central goals.

Comprehensive Technical Assistance to Support Program Outcomes

Carrie Farmer (RAND Corporation) offered reflections on the role of technical assistance as a strategic tool for helping community-based programs monitor their performance and achieve success. Echoing earlier remarks, Farmer noted that grantees and community-based organizations can have mixed capacities for data collection, evaluation, and reporting depending on how big or small they are; availability of financial,

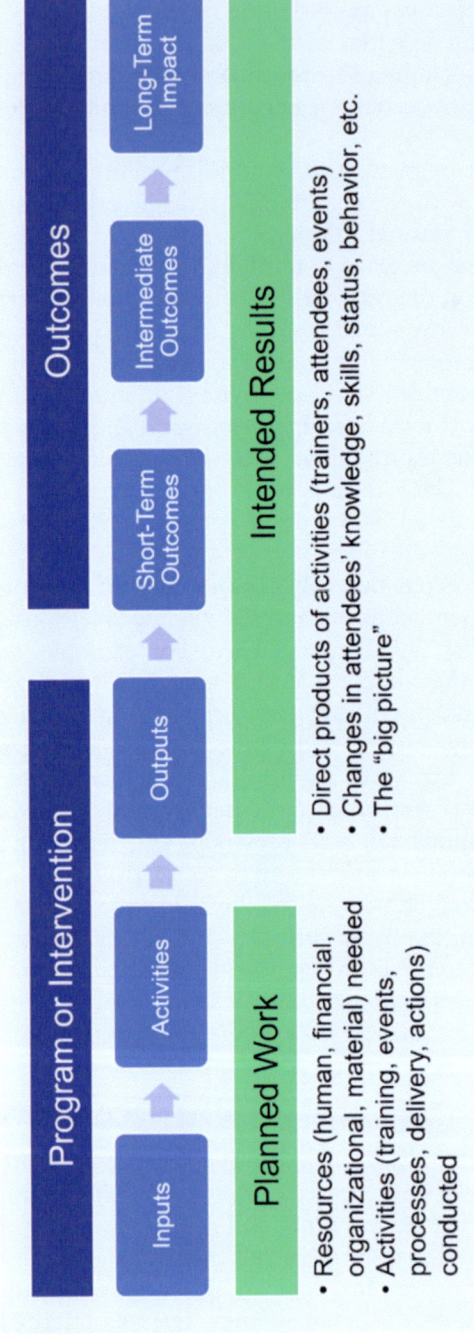

FIGURE 3-11 Logic model layout and terminology.
SOURCE: Presentation by Corbin Standley on April 29, 2025; American Foundation for Suicide Prevention.

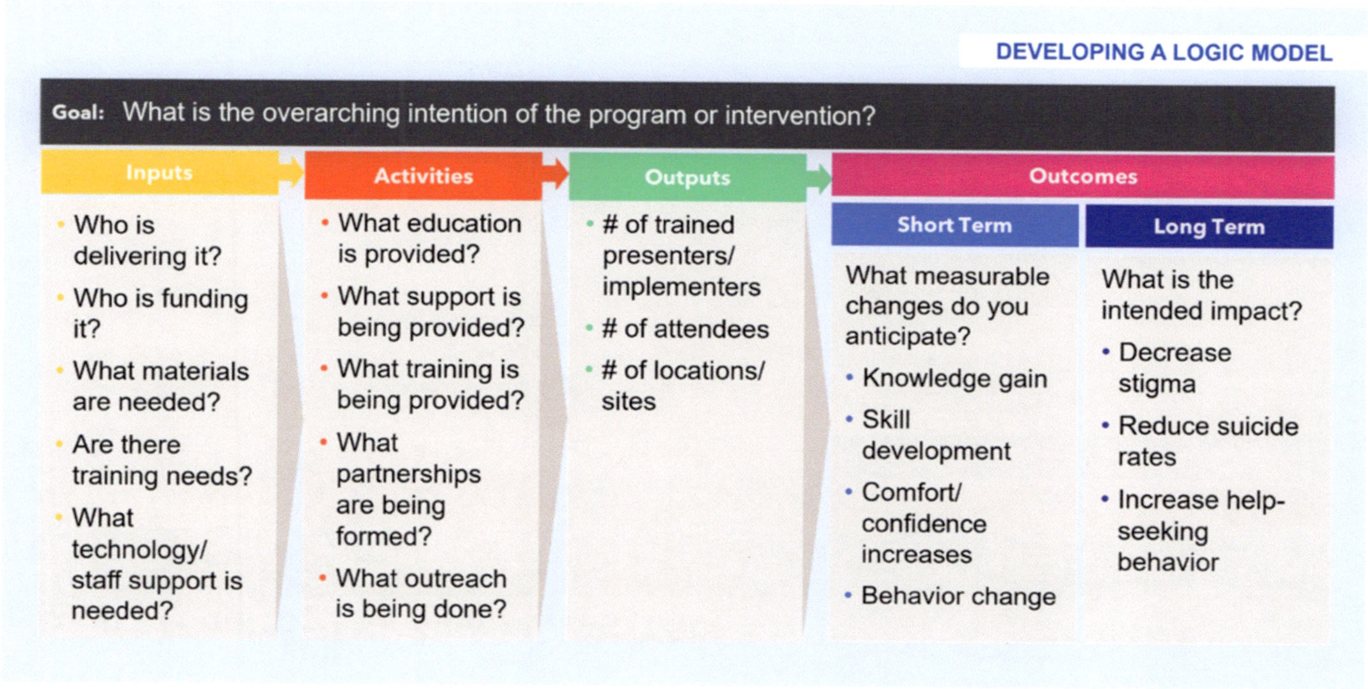

DEVELOPING A LOGIC MODEL

Goal: What is the overarching intention of the program or intervention?

Inputs	Activities	Outputs	Outcomes	
			Short Term	**Long Term**
• Who is delivering it? • Who is funding it? • What materials are needed? • Are there training needs? • What technology/staff support is needed?	• What education is provided? • What support is being provided? • What training is being provided? • What partnerships are being formed? • What outreach is being done?	• # of trained presenters/implementers • # of attendees • # of locations/sites	What measurable changes do you anticipate? • Knowledge gain • Skill development • Comfort/confidence increases • Behavior change	What is the intended impact? • Decrease stigma • Reduce suicide rates • Increase help-seeking behavior

FIGURE 3-12A Logic model development and example.
SOURCE: Presentation by Corbin Standley on April 29, 2025; American Foundation for Suicide Prevention.

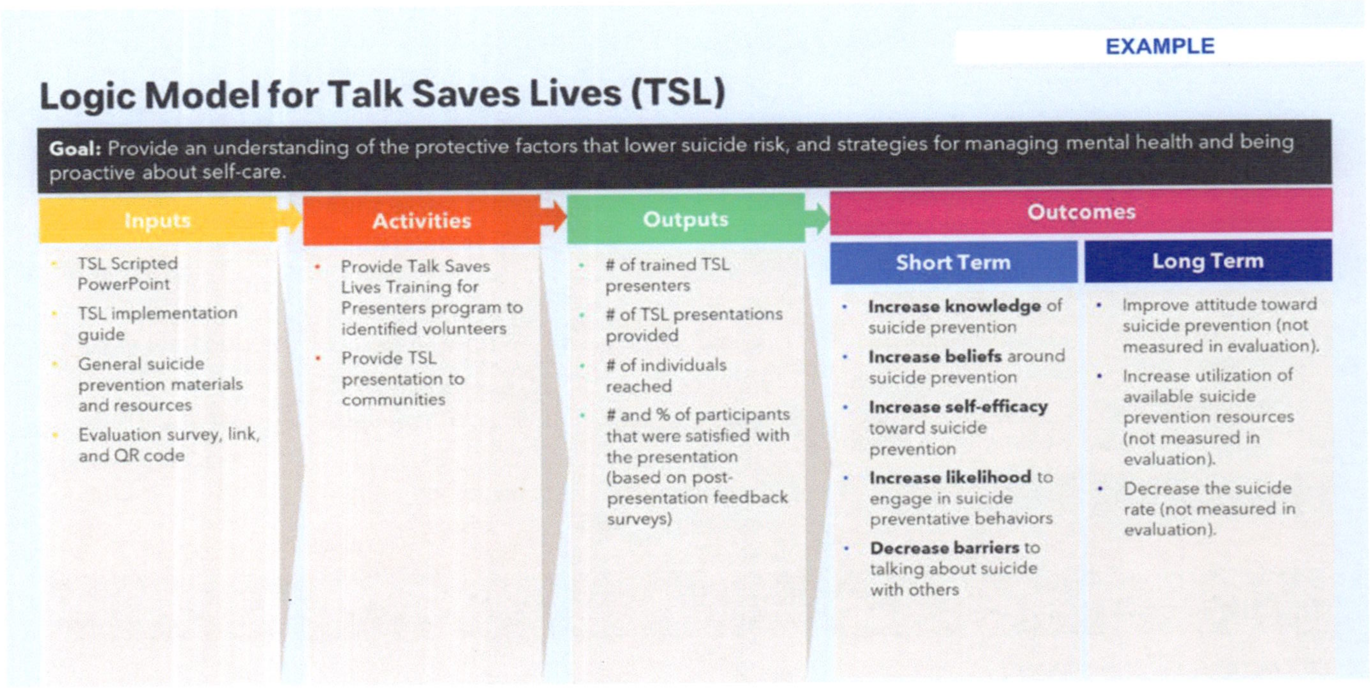

Logic Model for Talk Saves Lives (TSL)

Goal: Provide an understanding of the protective factors that lower suicide risk, and strategies for managing mental health and being proactive about self-care.

EXAMPLE

Inputs
- TSL Scripted PowerPoint
- TSL implementation guide
- General suicide prevention materials and resources
- Evaluation survey, link, and QR code

Activities
- Provide Talk Saves Lives Training for Presenters program to identified volunteers
- Provide TSL presentation to communities

Outputs
- # of trained TSL presenters
- # of TSL presentations provided
- # of individuals reached
- # and % of participants that were satisfied with the presentation (based on post-presentation feedback surveys)

Outcomes

Short Term
- **Increase knowledge** of suicide prevention
- **Increase beliefs** around suicide prevention
- **Increase self-efficacy** toward suicide prevention
- **Increase likelihood** to engage in suicide preventative behaviors
- **Decrease barriers** to talking about suicide with others

Long Term
- Improve attitude toward suicide prevention (not measured in evaluation).
- Increase utilization of available suicide prevention resources (not measured in evaluation).
- Decrease the suicide rate (not measured in evaluation).

FIGURE 3-12B Logic model development and example.
SOURCE: Presentation by Corbin Standley on April 29, 2025; American Foundation for Suicide Prevention.

technological, and other resources; staff expertise; and connections to other expertise.

Farmer explained that traditional technical assistance typically involves providing on-demand assistance for specific problems as they arise over the course of program design, implementation, and evaluation. In contrast, comprehensive technical assistance is more proactive and takes a long-term approach, with a goal of building knowledge and capacity for grantees to collect and evaluate outcomes on their own, thus reducing their reliance on technical assistance in the future.

A comprehensive approach can help align grantees around the measurement of priority outcomes the funder is interested in, thus ensuring relevant data are collected, Farmer noted. It can also build a cohort of programs or grantees so they can learn from each other and share best practices. Comprehensive technical assistance may include one-on-one coaching, in-depth assessment of grantee needs, development of individualized support plans, and active tracking of grantee progress over time.

Farmer pointed to the technical assistance provided by SAMHSA's Service Members, Veterans, and their Families (SMVF) Technical Assistance Center[3] as a promising comprehensive support model (see Figure 3-13). She described what is entailed in each of the model's four phases:

1. Phase 1 focuses on orienting each grantee to the intervention through a cohort-based model that ensures fidelity to the program's core components. This phase emphasizes level-setting and understanding the context of each specific grantee.
2. Phase 2 consists of a series of web-based preparatory sessions that introduce foundational concepts. Through presentations by subject matter experts, grantees receive structured education on key topics such as evidence-based practices, logic model development, and data management—including how to collect, interpret, and store data effectively.
3. Phase 3 brings grantees together for an Implementation Academy. During the Academy, grantees deepen their understanding of the specific issue(s) they are working to address, strengthen their ability to implement it successfully, and learn from lessons shared by peers and experts. This phase helps organizations identify suitable evidence-based practices, understand implementation challenges, and develop strategic implementation plans.

---

[3] The Service Members, Veterans, and their Families Technical Assistance Center (https://www.samhsa.gov/technical-assistance/smvf), supported by SAMHSA, acts as a national resource that helps states, territories, tribes, and local communities build their capacity to meet the behavioral health needs of military and veteran families.

FIGURE 3-13 Comprehensive technical assistance example.
NOTE: SAMHSA = Substance Abuse and Mental Health Services Administration.
SOURCE: Presentation by Carrie Farmer on April 29, 2025; SAMHSA Service Members.

CONSIDERATIONS FOR PROGRAM DEVELOPMENT AND OVERSIGHT 47

4. Phase 4 consists of individualized technical assistance. This ongoing support helps grantees troubleshoot challenges, adapt practices as needed, and sustain implementation quality over time.

Farmer underscored the value of the model's heavy focus on implementation, noting that desired outcomes will not be achieved if the intervention is not implemented well from the start.

Service Members, Veterans, and Their Families Technical Assistance Center

The SMVF Technical Assistance Center's approach to comprehensive technical assistance might serve as a useful model for the Sergeant Parker Gordon Fox Suicide Prevention Grant Program, Farmer noted. She suggested several specific elements that could strengthen the Fox program's technical assistance approach. These include offering virtual workshops on topics such as evaluation design, data collection, data analysis, and communication. Farmer emphasized the importance of one-on-one technical assistance, as grantee needs can vary widely—some organizations may require support in identifying appropriate metrics, while others may need guidance in navigating institutional review board processes. She also recommended the development of evaluation support tools, such as a curated catalogue of process and outcome measures, as well as the creation of a community of practice that would allow grantees to learn from one another.

Design of Actionable Dashboards for Supporting Program Implementation and Oversight

Itzhak Yanovitzky (Rutgers University) provided an overview of how dashboards can serve as actionable tools in support of public health initiatives. Drawing from his expertise in behavioral and social change communication, he discussed how dashboards—when properly designed and implemented—can be leveraged not only for monitoring and dissemination but also for strategic planning, goal setting, coordination, and system learning.

He emphasized that while dashboards are often used to track program performance or report outcomes, they hold broader potential to advance decision-making and catalyze action. Actionable dashboards can permit real-time access to curated data, enable users to visualize trends and detect bottlenecks, support implementation decisions, and connect stakeholders across systems. As illustrated in Figure 3-14, dashboard design involves a range of decisions regarding data, users, and purpose—from monitoring and communication to alignment and learning.

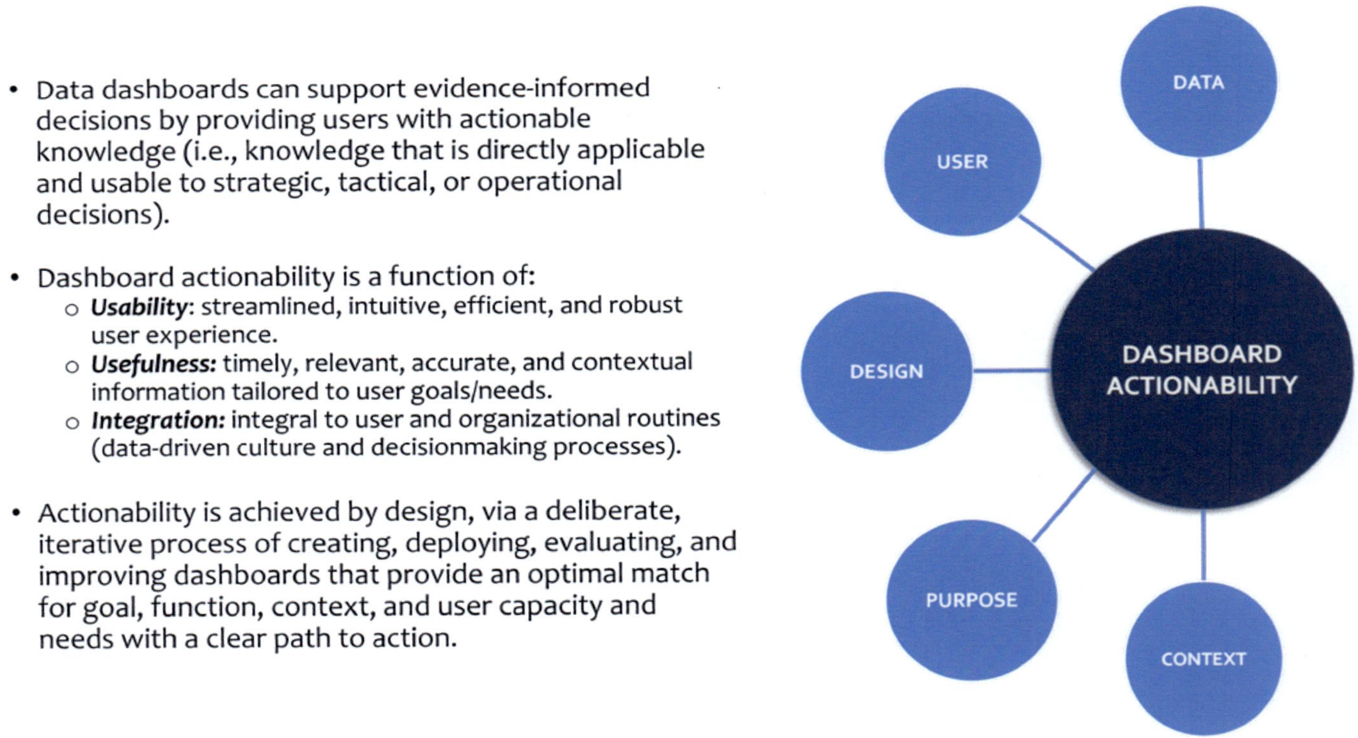

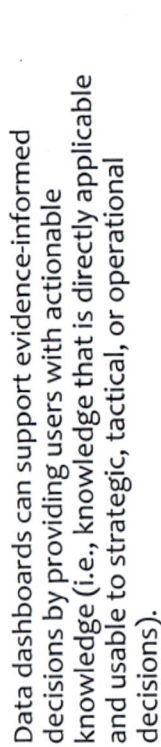

• Data dashboards can support evidence-informed decisions by providing users with actionable knowledge (i.e., knowledge that is directly applicable and usable to strategic, tactical, or operational decisions).
• Dashboard actionability is a function of:
o *Usability*: streamlined, intuitive, efficient, and robust user experience.
o *Usefulness:* timely, relevant, accurate, and contextual information tailored to user goals/needs.
o *Integration:* integral to user and organizational routines (data-driven culture and decisionmaking processes).
• Actionability is achieved by design, via a deliberate, iterative process of creating, deploying, evaluating, and improving dashboards that provide an optimal match for goal, function, context, and user capacity and needs with a clear path to action.
DATA
USER
DESIGN
DASHBOARD ACTIONABILITY
PURPOSE
CONTEXT

FIGURE 3-14 Data dashboard actionability.
SOURCE: Presentation by Itzhak Yanovitzky on April 29, 2025.

However, Yanovitzky cautioned that building a dashboard alone does not guarantee its usefulness or use. Simply providing access to data does not mean people will use it—or use it well. He outlined several factors that determine whether a dashboard actually influences behavior or supports action. These include the characteristics of the data itself (e.g., timeliness, granularity), user capacity and needs, the purpose of the dashboard (strategic vs. tactical), the design elements (interactivity, customization), the context in which the dashboard is being introduced (e.g., policy environment, user norms), and whether it is integrated into existing workflows.

Dashboards, Yanovitzky noted, often fail when developed in isolation from their intended users. To overcome this challenge, he proposed an "actionability by design" approach—a process that brings together program staff, data scientists, and end users to co-create dashboards that meet real-world needs and achieve three overlapping goals: usability, usefulness, and integration (see Figure 3-15). Yanovitzky explained that usability refers to whether a dashboard is intuitive, efficient, and accessible. Usefulness reflects whether it delivers timely, context-relevant information that supports decision-making. Integration requires that dashboards become embedded into daily workflows and organizational culture. If a dashboard is not used consistently, it will not achieve its intended purpose, he stated.

Yanovitzky described "actionability by design" as a collaborative, iterative process that begins with identifying shared problems and mapping pathways for action. From there, the team defines data needs, develops the dashboard collaboratively, and periodically refines it while addressing potential unintended consequences.

Yanovitzky also stressed that dashboards must be tailored to the specific context and application; they are not templates. He shared a concrete example from New Jersey, where a statewide opioid dashboard was developed through inter-agency collaboration. The project began with public town halls and evolved into a tool that allowed for cross-county learning, resource mapping, and alignment of services across government systems. He concluded his presentation by reiterating that such an impact is only possible when the dashboard design process is grounded in early and sustained collaboration with stakeholders.

PANEL DISCUSSIONS AND AUDIENCE Q&A

After the foundational presentations, the session moved to a series of two moderated panel discussions. The first panel discussion focused on lessons learned from the examples of programs supporting non-clinical community-based suicide prevention efforts discussed earlier in the day. The second panel discussion provided the opportunity for other invited experts to offer additional insights. Audience Q&A followed the panel discussions.

FIGURE 3-15 Actionability as a design process.
SOURCE: Presentation by Itzhak Yanovitzky on April 29, 2025.

Lessons Learned from Examples of Non-Clinical Community-Based Suicide Prevention Efforts

Colin Walsh (Vanderbilt University; member, workshop planning committee) served as moderator for both panel discussions summarized in this chapter. The first panel discussion was with the individuals who had given the presentations summarized in Chapter 2: Mary Cwik (Johns Hopkins University), Novalene Alsenay Goklish (Johns Hopkins University), Brandi Jancaitis (Virginia Department of Veterans Services), Richard McKeon (SAMHSA), and David Rozek (University of Texas Health Science Center at San Antonio). Topics included structuring programs to minimize grantee burden, fostering collaboration and peer learning, tailoring outreach and respecting community readiness, planning for evaluation and communication of findings, and reflections on grant design and adaptation.

Structuring Programs to Minimize Grantee Burden

Walsh began the moderated panel discussion by asking panelists to share lessons learned around how to structure programs to minimize burden on grantees. Jancaitis noted that this is an important question that she and her team grapple with daily. As their grant sizes are relatively small ($75,000 to $175,000 per grantee, which may barely fund a full-time staff member depending on level of staffing), grantees have to be creative in how they use that investment. Jancaitis added that the small awards drew grantees that might have smaller infrastructures, so expectations for impact needed to be realistic. She noted that they begin providing technical assistance before the grant is awarded to help grantees with awareness of resources and where to go for data to help define the need, as well as capacity to put together a basic logic model. In addition to pointing to best practices, technical assistance providers answered questions as prospective grantees put together their applications and continued to layer resourcing in between their reporting cycles. Jancaitis emphasized that a core lesson learned was that technical assistance has to start from the beginning and continue throughout the program.

Rozek also commented on the work that is needed to support prospective grantees prior to receiving an award. He and his team approach support for prospective grantees as building a partnership and examining how they might help with infrastructure or barriers to starting the work. As an example of the latter, he noted that some organizations might have hiring restrictions that require funding to have been received before a position can be posted. Given that there might be a lag time of three months or more between the start of the grant period and receipt of funding, this can present challenges if funding is not for a multi-year period. Rozek noted that they will work with grantees to scope out an appropriate initial project from which they can build capacity into potential future funding cycles or grant opportunities, thus setting up organizations for success. Additionally, the first grant to an organization may be focused on building or strengthening their infrastructure; the outcomes of that infrastructure grant will not be an immediate large-scale impact, he stated, but it will enable an organization to hire key staff and build out programmatic areas, which Face the Fight views as important progress and can set the organization up for larger and more lasting impact over time.

Making sure the grant truly supports what communities want to do is first and foremost, Cwik added, so it is critical to get community input on how these grants are structured. Community partners should be involved in shaping reporting requirements and data collection, so they understand why funders want that information; this helps teams to get on board with the burden of gathering that information. Cwik stated that reporting is an area where they provide a lot of technical assistance to support, because teams want to be out there helping community members at risk for suicide, rather than focusing time on grant reports. Their technical assistance providers try to reduce the reporting burden. She also stressed the importance of offering flexibility with requirements where possible, as well as grant officers and communities working collaboratively.

Goklish added that grant coordinators and managers based in small rural communities may have to be creative in meeting a grant's goals and objectives. As an example, she noted that sometimes a tribe may not be willing to share certain data; in such instances, the grant manager has to determine what can be reported on instead. They often start by doing a small pilot of a program before implementing it on a wider scale; this helps with ensuring that staff understand the goals and objectives, how to relay those goals and objectives to the community members they are working to help, and how to move the program forward, Goklish noted. When a program is struggling initially, they take stock of whether the program aligns with community interest and what changes may be needed to improve the alignment.

For the GLS program, there were grant requirements that were not under the control of the program staff, so their focus was on providing support and building a sense of team with grantees, rather than reducing burden, McKeon explained. At the start of the GLS program, each grantee had a person from SPRC assigned to them to provide technical assistance. A member of the evaluation team also participated on each call with grantees.

Fostering Collaboration and Peer Learning

Several panel members commented on the importance of fostering collaboration and peer learning. Building on his remarks about supporting grantees through robust technical assistance, McKeon stated that another support strategy employed at GLS is convening grantees together for in-person meetings to facilitate peer learning and information exchange. These meetings provide opportunities outside of the formal evaluation process for grantees to identify and share early successes.

Jancaitis noted that fostering a sense of community among grantees is a focus of the Virginia Department of Veterans Services Suicide Prevention and Opioid Addiction Services program, too. In addition to hosting biannual symposiums for training and networking, the program supports ongoing connection through a grantee newsletter and regular "lunch and learn" sessions.

Rozek emphasized the value of connecting organizations that are doing similar work but may not be aware of one another. He noted that there are lots of groups engaged in very similar efforts—sometimes even using the same terminology—but they are not in conversation. Geographic separation or limited visibility can prevent collaboration, even among groups facing comparable challenges. Facilitating those connections, Rozek suggested, can significantly increase collective impact. Sharing resources can help everyone avoid reinventing the wheel and make each investment go further.

He added that fostering a sense of community among grantees also improves the effectiveness of technical assistance. "We can troubleshoot the same problems a hundred times in a hundred organizations," Rozek noted, and connecting grantees facing similar barriers and letting them learn from each other can result in more effective problem solving than what is achievable from technical assistance alone. He observed that peer knowledge-sharing has been particularly valuable when organizations have already overcome specific barriers and are willing to share what worked.

Rozek also spoke to the importance of facilitating connection not just among grantees, but between grantees and the broader Face the Fight coalition. "We have a coalition side," he explained, "and we want our grantees and others doing really amazing work to share ideas, interventions, and programming." While he acknowledged that suicide prevention is rarely a "one size fits all" endeavor, Rozek emphasized that programs can often be adapted when there is shared interest or alignment. They have had many cases where they have played "matchmaker" between organizations, such as a case where they connected a financial services group that wanted to implement universal screening but was unsure how to respond to a positive screen with another group already doing that work. Such connections, Rozek added, often emerge only because funders, technical assistance teams, and coalition members are all attuned to common needs and challenges across organizations.

Tailoring Outreach and Respecting Community Readiness

Walsh commented on the emerging themes of the cyclical or iterative nature of assistance and support, identifying barriers directly with grantees and working creatively to overcome them, and shaping programs in partnership with grantees. These themes, he noted, offered a useful lead-in to the next question—how to cultivate applicants, particularly in communities that programs may want to reach but that have not historically received strong support for efforts of this kind.

McKeon reflected on the early days of the GLS program and the landscape of suicide prevention at the time it was launched. "You have to understand what the environment was like back in 2004," he said. "Garrett Lee Smith was the first nationally available funding source for suicide prevention in the United States, so there was a hunger for resources in states and communities across the country." At that time, eligible applicants included states, tribes, and their designees. McKeon noted that states quickly became aware of the opportunity, in part due to infrastructure already in place through SPRC's contact with state suicide prevention coordinators. Additional effort was needed to raise awareness among tribal communities, however, he added, requiring explicit attention as the program moved forward.

For the Face the Fight initiative, understanding the current suicide prevention landscape was seen as important to informing their work, Rozek stated. They provided a grant to the RAND Corporation to conduct a landscape analysis for current and emerging work in this area, which was released just prior to the workshop (Ramchand et al., 2025). This analysis will equip Face the Fight to identify potentially scalable programs that may be a fit for their mission.

Jancaitis responded that the organizations her team seeks to bring into the funding portfolio generally fall into two broad categories. The first group is deeply embedded in the military community, with strong military culture and military- or veteran-connected staff. While these organizations tend to be well positioned to serve veteran populations, they may need additional support in areas such as mental health, suicide prevention, and integration with broader service systems. The second group consists of more mainstream organizations with well-established mental health programming but limited experience working with military-connected populations.

Military bases and other military facilities are one possible avenue for reaching the former community, Jancaitis noted, but it is important to consider community needs and approach with cultural sensitivity, particularly in populations where help-seeking can be particularly difficult or even taboo.

Another point Jancaitis emphasized was that outreach and marketing are often undervalued by funders. "You can't build it and assume they will come," she said, particularly when working with populations where help-seeking may be difficult. Now working in a funding role herself, Jancaitis acknowledged the tension funders face, but stressed the importance of integrating outreach into the life cycle of a grant from the outset.

Cwik and Goklish emphasized the importance of cultural sensitivity in thinking about outreach. Cwik noted that they represent a university-community partnership, and while there are other tribes that could be strong candidates to carry out similar work to that of the White Mountain Apache Tribe, their approach has been to share their work in forums that include participants from tribal communities, rather than reaching out to specific communities directly. She added that she does not want to be seen as a university-based researcher pushing what might be perceived as her agenda or her center's agenda onto another community. Goklish explained that their team does not proactively approach other tribes because, as outsiders, they do not want to imply that a community is struggling with suicide or make assumptions about its needs. "The only time we approach a tribe," she said, "is if they've already reached out to us and we are aware of their situation."

When another tribe expresses interest in the Celebrating Life program, Goklish's team is open to collaboration but emphasizes the importance of meeting communities where they are. She underscored that there is no "quick fix" for suicide prevention. "We do not have a happy pill," she said. "We do not have a program that will fix it all overnight." It took years to build the White Mountain Apache program, Goklish noted, and other communities should expect a similarly gradual process. She emphasized the importance of starting from the beginning—working closely with the community to implement an approach that is both effective and culturally sensitive. She noted that in many Native American communities, suicide remains a taboo subject, making it especially important to secure support from tribal Elders and leaders in order to move the work forward. Goklish added that her team makes a point of sharing this perspective with communities that reach out. "Sometimes they are not happy about what we have to say," she acknowledged, "but we believe in being transparent—sharing what we struggled with and why it is important to have community support in place before implementing anything."

Planning for Evaluation and Communication of Findings

Walsh asked panel members to share insights and lessons learned related to determining the appropriate level of budget and other resources to allocate to evaluation and monitoring. Rozek responded that the appropriate level of budget and resources for evaluation often depends on an organization's existing infrastructure and capacity. Some of it starts with understanding how much data is already being collected, what internal expertise exists, and what resources are currently in place, he explained. The more funders and technical assistance providers know about an organization's baseline capacity, the better they can support the development of an appropriate evaluation budget. Rozek emphasized that the process often begins with building infrastructure tailored to the organization's current needs, with an eye toward scaling that capacity to meet future evaluation expectations.

Jancaitis mused that she did not have a "magic answer" about the percentage of funding to allocate for evaluation, but, as with outreach, it is important to present it as part of the life cycle of a grant from the beginning. Cwik added that evaluation and monitoring always takes more time and person-effort than is expected. Planning for data analysis to take place in the last month of a grant is not sufficient; data analysis should be put earlier in the timeline.

Thinking in terms of effective resource use, McKeon stated, "If you're collecting data, use the data. Don't collect data you don't need or that you can't use in the very near future to do the work." This principle reflects a broader theme raised by several panelists: evaluation should be designed not just for funders, but to inform real-time program improvement and support decision-making at the grantee level.

Additional Reflections on Grant Design and Adaptation

Expanding on a point he raised during his presentation, McKeon reflected on lessons learned from the original design of the Garrett Lee Smith (GLS) grant program and how those insights informed changes to its structure over time. The program initially funded three-year grants, but grantees reported that the effective implementation window was significantly compressed. The first year is often spent gearing up, McKeon explained, and the third year is focused on preparing to close out, which really leaves only one solid year for deep implementation. In addition, mortality data suggested that while some GLS-funded interventions were having an impact, those effects tended to fade after the grant period ended. To address these challenges, the grant model was revised. Rather than awarding $400,000 per year for three years ($1.2 million total), the program began offering five-year grants totaling $3.6 million—effectively tripling the available funding over a longer time horizon. McKeon noted that this adjustment appeared to yield stronger and more sustainable results, as reflected in subsequent evaluation data.

McKeon added that elements of the GLS program required grantees to stretch. As an example, he cited the Early Identification Referral Form (ERIF), a tool introduced as part of the evaluation strategy to track whether youth identified as at risk through screening or gatekeeper training actually received the care they needed. Implementing ERIF was not easy, he acknowledged, as many communities lacked systems for tracking follow-up care. Still, the program team believed it was worth the effort. They needed to do more than just gather information from gatekeepers for the purpose of evaluation in order to know what happened to the young people who had been identified as at risk.

These reflections on grant design underscore the evolving nature of program implementation and evaluation, as well as the need for continuous learning across the field. As McKeon noted, building and sustaining a national infrastructure for suicide prevention requires not only funding and strategy, but a community of practice committed to sharing progress and growing together. "When I started in suicide prevention in 2001 or 2002," he recalled, "most of the people working in the field could fit in a single room and there would be plenty of space." He contrasted that with the present-day reality, where national conferences regularly draw over a thousand attendees. "We have built a workforce and a community," he said. "There is reason for hope, because many programs have shown forward progress and impact." He emphasized the importance of continuing to learn from one another, noting that gatherings like the workshop offer essential opportunities to do just that.

Expert Insights on Program Development and Oversight and Grantee-Level Implementation and Performance Metrics

During the second panel discussion, the speakers who provided the foundational presentations summarized above were joined by Ebony Akinsanya (Centers for Disease Control and Prevention [CDC] Foundation) and Christine Walrath (ICF) to discuss topics including encouraging applications and assessing application quality; criteria for determining participant eligibility; best practices for outreach and soliciting participation; and best practices for data collection, use, and infrastructure.

Encouraging Applications and Assessing Application Quality

Walsh invited panelists to reflect on ways to expand access to and awareness of grant funding and to encourage applications, particularly among organizations that may not traditionally apply or see themselves as part of the public health space. Akinsanya responded by noting that the CDC Foundation has administered a mini-grant program for the past seven years that provides evaluation, capacity building, and technical assistance to veteran-serving organizations. Participating organizations are required to implement interventions aligned with protective or risk-reducing strategies identified in CDC's Suicide Prevention Resource for Action. One lesson learned from the program is the importance of working with veteran-serving organizations to help them recognize their public health role and build their confidence to apply for funding. She noted that some organizations do not readily see themselves as candidates for suicide prevention work and that funders can help bridge that gap. "She emphasized that outreach and encouragement are essential, along with keeping application barriers low. For example, her organization has moved away from requesting demonstration of evaluation experience as part of the application process; this experience is no longer expected of applicants.

Crosby encouraged programs to think about outreach to organizations that might have veteran community connections but may not recognize their work as relevant to suicide prevention. Stout added that state veteran service agencies may also be good avenues for spreading the word about funding opportunities to more local networks, along with state suicide prevention leads, who are often connected with many community coalitions. She also called attention to the Suicide Prevention Resource Center (SPRC) Best Practices Registry,[4] which offers a valuable resource for identifying interventions that reflect a broader range of evidence and emphasize inclusivity, cultural relevance, and population diversity. Standley echoed the value of the SPRC Best Practices Registry as a resource.

In terms of assessing applicant quality, Farmer suggested programs may want to consider having different criteria for different types of applicants. For example, if a prospective grantee is proposing an activity that is a new idea for which there is not a lot of evidence, maybe that would be more of a research grant to help build that evidence. If a prospective grantee has limited capacity, programs may want to emulate Face the Fight's approach and treat it as more of an implementation grant to help build that capacity. Grants to established organizations that have a lot more experience may be treated as expansion grants. In other words, Farmer continued, programs may want to have different criteria for applications that would be dependent on the goals and the capabilities of the organizations applying to the program.

Walrath added that programs need to consider that capacity building requires sufficient resource allocation to ensure grantees are adequately equipped for both implementation and participation in evaluation. She also encouraged programs to ensure that they are selecting grantees who are committed to participating in evaluation and data collection, as well as committed to using data to inform their own improvement over time.

Yanovitzky added that funders can play a more active role in expanding access by using a combination of "push and pull" strategies that leverage

---

[4] https://bpr.sprc.org/

relationships, partnerships, and existing networks. For example, grantees themselves can be engaged as trusted messengers to help bring new voices, particularly early-career scholars, into the field. This approach broadens the reach of funding opportunities and helps avoid insular "echo chambers," he said. He emphasized that understanding the broader ecosystem of actors in suicide prevention and meeting potential applicants "where they are" can help build trust and spark interest among organizations that might not otherwise seek out funding. Yanovitzky pointed to a recent example in which the Robert Wood Johnson Foundation launched a rapid-response funding opportunity and asked established partners to disseminate the information through targeted, relationship-based channels to accelerate uptake. Funders, he concluded, should be more proactive and deliberate in how they share opportunities and engage prospective applicants.

Criteria for Determining Participant Eligibility

Walsh then turned the discussion to the individuals these programs are ultimately intended to serve. He asked panelists what criteria they would recommend for determining who should be eligible to participate in the community-based suicide prevention programs offered by grantees. Stout responded that, based on her experience serving on the planning committee and thinking deeply about community-based suicide prevention, over-inclusion is generally appropriate for these types of programs. Using the example of the GLS program, which has a targeted age range for youth suicide prevention and also prioritizes groups at disproportionate risk, she emphasized the importance of casting a wide net. Drawing on the public health framework of universal, selective, and indicated interventions, she argued that upstream, strength-building programs should be designed to reach all individuals who are eligible under a given grant, not just those already known to be at elevated risk. Limiting participation to individuals already identified as at risk, she explained, may undercut the potential impact of community approaches. Referring to earlier points raised about upstream prevention, Stout stressed the evidence base supporting efforts to intervene early—"before individuals are at the edge of the waterfall"—because reaching people upstream is where community approaches are going to be most impactful. At the same time, she acknowledged the importance of also developing programming for populations known to be at higher risk and ensuring crisis supports are available for those in acute distress. This inclusive approach, she said, is distinct from the structure of a closed clinical system, which typically focuses on indicated populations already engaged in treatment.

Yanovitzky added that while public health typically relies on identified needs to inform program development and targeting—particularly when groups are not being reached or are underengaged—he noted that readiness to change is also a critical factor. He explained that trying to engage individuals or groups who currently lack the capacity, motivation, or opportunity to act may be ineffective in the short term. Instead, focusing on those who are ready to take action can generate early momentum and produce a cascading or snowball effect, building broader engagement over time. In his experience, he said, striking a balance between need and readiness can help maximize near-term impact while setting the stage for long-term change.

Walsh concluded the discussion of the question of eligibility criteria by underscoring the importance of both assessing need and gauging readiness when determining program eligibility. He emphasized that effective community-based suicide prevention requires meeting individuals and communities where they are—both in terms of risk and readiness for change.

Best Practices for Outreach and Soliciting Participation

To continue the conversation around reaching those most likely to benefit from suicide prevention services, Walsh invited panelists to offer recommendations for how grantees can best disseminate information about their services and encourage participation. He invited them to reflect on strategies that have proven effective for building awareness and increasing engagement among the populations that grantees seek to serve.

Standley opened the discussion by emphasizing the importance of identifying trusted community members—both formal and informal leaders—who can help spread awareness. These individuals might include local business owners, parks and recreation staff, or shelter workers. He encouraged expanding traditional definitions of leadership and expertise to include those with lived experience, such as loss survivors, attempt survivors, or those deeply engaged in schools or other community systems. Building relationships with trusted community figures, Standley noted, can help generate a snowball effect that broadens the reach of outreach efforts.

Crosby echoed these points, highlighting the importance of identifying both formal and informal community leaders. He recalled a story about a senator who disclosed personal experience with suicide loss in a public setting for the first time, underscoring the potential influence of public figures who choose to speak out. Crosby also noted the importance of ensuring that community stakeholders and program participants receive information about the work being done, creating a feedback loop that helps generate buy-in and build goodwill.

Stout added that community engagement is a two-way street: it is not only about disseminating information but also about learning from others engaged in related work. She encouraged grantees to ask what community leaders and partners are already doing, how their efforts may align with suicide prevention, and where there may be opportunities to support or build upon existing initiatives.

Yanovitzky emphasized that both communication and evaluation should be treated as integral to program planning and implementation, not afterthoughts. He urged grantees and funders to engage experts in communication and dissemination science early in the process and to build adequate funding into program budgets for these activities. Effective dissemination, he explained, requires careful planning, audience analysis, and clear strategies for engagement and message delivery. He noted that without this, programs risk missing the opportunity to communicate impact in ways that resonate and inspire action.

Akinsanya shared that, in the fourth year of her program, grantees were required to develop communication and dissemination plans. These were built on earlier efforts to create partner engagement plans and to understand the expectations of various stakeholders. She explained that effective dissemination requires tailoring findings to meet the needs of different audiences, and that grantees should be encouraged to share results publicly—through conference presentations, white papers, or other formats—regardless of whether they come from traditional academic backgrounds.

Farmer agreed, adding that the ability of an organization to engage its community should be considered during the grant application process. Programs should assess the degree to which applicants are embedded in and connected to the communities they propose to serve. If an applicant lacks that capacity, she said, funders should ensure that resources are provided to support meaningful community engagement. Without that connection, even well-intentioned efforts may fall flat or miss their intended audience.

Standley returned to the importance of evaluating the partnerships themselves. He noted that when programs fall short of expected outcomes, it may be because the partnerships underlying the work are not functioning optimally. Evaluating partnership processes—such as levels of trust, alignment on goals, and perceptions of sustainability—can help identify areas for improvement and ensure that partnerships remain strong and effective throughout and beyond the funding period.

Crosby closed the discussion by emphasizing the value of peer-to-peer learning among grantees. He observed that funders can help facilitate this exchange by convening grantees to share their strategies and experiences. In such settings, participants can learn from one another, adopt successful approaches, and strengthen their own community engagement efforts as a result.

Strengthening Data Capacity: Best Practices for Collection, Use, and Infrastructure

For the final question of the panel discussion, Walsh invited panelists to share best practices for supporting grantees in handling data, a central cross-cutting theme of the workshop. He asked them to reflect on topics such as identifying common data elements, using data repositories, and building capacity for meaningful use and interpretation.

Walrath opened the discussion by highlighting the value of common data elements across grant programs. She stressed that common data elements do not imply inflexibility, but rather a baseline that supports both local and cross-site evaluation while allowing room for additional, tailored measures. Walrath emphasized the importance of collecting and analyzing implementation data alongside outcomes, explaining that without a clear understanding of what was delivered and at what scale, impact is difficult to interpret. She also shared an example from the GLS program, which uses a centralized data repository that allows all grantees to enter and access data within a shared system. While such infrastructure requires resources, Walrath noted, it offers substantial benefits in terms of consistency, accessibility, and insight.

Crosby expanded on the idea of core data elements, drawing on examples from infectious disease reporting. He pointed to the CDC's system for weekly notifiable disease surveillance, where each state is required to report on a core data set but may also choose to add context-specific elements, and underscored the value of applying a similar model in suicide prevention—balancing national consistency with local flexibility. Crosby also emphasized the need for community sensitivity in data collection and cited the importance of ensuring that underserved populations are adequately represented. As an example, he noted early gaps in COVID-19 race and ethnicity data that limited the ability to tailor effective interventions. He urged suicide prevention programs to collect complete and representative data to avoid similar blind spots.

Yanovitzky offered three additional considerations. First, he emphasized that data should be actionable; they must be collected and used in support of decision-making and learning. Second, he encouraged programs to expand their definition of impact to include broader elements such as capacity-building, and to engage stakeholders in shaping how that impact is defined and measured. Third, he underscored the opportunity to build data infrastructure across communities and programs. He shared that, in his own work, data repositories are a requirement of foundation-funded grants, and that universities can often support long-term public access. He advocated for open data platforms and cross-state collaboration, noting the potential to create valuable shared resources that do not currently exist at the federal level.

Akinsanya added that both qualitative and quantitative data should be recognized as important. In her program's federally funded work, they often rely on qualitative data from grantees due to restrictions on other forms of data collection. Grantees have reported that their involvement in evaluation has strengthened community partnerships, increased program credibility, improved services for veterans, and enhanced organizational viability. These outcomes, she emphasized, reflect meaningful benefits that may not be captured through quantitative indicators alone.

Walrath returned to the conversation to emphasize two final points: first, that programs should avoid duplicative data collection by leveraging existing sources when available, and second, that data should only be collected if they will be used. She reiterated that limited resources should be focused on generating useful, actionable insights that inform practice.

Audience Q&A

Walsh offered audience members the opportunity to ask questions of participants from both panels. Topics raised by audience members included clarifying program goals to inform data collection, inclusion criteria for community-based programs, finding funding and collaborative partners, and supporting community engagement in the pre-award phase.

Clarifying Program Goals to Inform Data Collection

Tanha Patel (CDC Foundation) raised a point about the importance of clarifying a program's intent before establishing data collection protocols. While much of the discussion had centered on common data elements, she emphasized that without a clear understanding of a funder's goals, it is difficult to determine which data are meaningful. Stout agreed, suggesting that just as grantees are expected to develop logic models, funders should do the same. These models can help define expected short- and intermediate-term outcomes and guide evaluation planning. Farmer added that upfront alignment between data needs at the program and grantee levels can help reduce burden while ensuring data are useful for both local and aggregate evaluation. Yanovitzky echoed the importance of feedback loops in this process. Too often, he said, grantees are treated like contractors, with little opportunity to shape future research agendas. Instead, funders should systematically gather grantee insights—such as through "exit polling"—to inform future funding priorities.

Inclusion Criteria for Community-Based Programs

The conversation then turned to screening tools and eligibility criteria. Michelle Kuntz (U.S. Department of Veterans Affairs Office of Suicide

Prevention) asked whether panelists had recommendations for identifying appropriate participants for upstream, non-clinical suicide prevention efforts. Stout emphasized the value of broad inclusion criteria, especially for veteran populations. While targeted screening tools may be appropriate in some cases, she cautioned that relying solely on clinical tools risks missing individuals who do not meet diagnostic thresholds but are still at risk. She added that from a public health perspective, overinclusion, especially for a veteran population, makes sense, noting that she would consider the whole veteran population as eligible for participation in community-based suicide prevention efforts. Askinaya agreed, stating that many at-risk veterans do not have clinical mental health diagnoses; instead, risk may stem from social factors like financial strain or relationship issues. Accordingly, her program does not impose strict screening requirements on grantees but does require demonstrated connections to the veteran community, she noted. Crosby encouraged attendees to think beyond veterans themselves, noting that family members—especially those who have experienced loss—may also face elevated risk and could be important targets for outreach and support.

Finding Funding and Collaborative Partners

Tina Winters (National Academies of Sciences, Engineering, and Medicine) noted that several virtual attendees—including one running a "vet café" in rural Oregon and others focused on peer support or combating isolation—were seeking guidance on where to find information about available funding and how to connect with potential collaborative partners. Jancaitis responded by acknowledging the challenge of identifying funding streams, particularly in the current climate of uncertainty. She suggested that state-level suicide prevention coalitions and the Governor's Challenge to Prevent Suicide could be valuable resources, as both typically bring together federal, state, and local funders. "Just the speakers that have been featured here gives you a good idea of the toolbox," she noted, encouraging participants to start by engaging with coalitions already active in their regions, even if they are not veteran specific.

Supporting Community Engagement in the Pre-Award Phase

Diana Clarke (American Psychiatric Association; member, workshop planning committee) posed a question to the panel related to funder flexibility and community engagement. She noted that while early engagement is critical for reaching the most vulnerable communities, those same communities often lack the time and resources to participate in program design before funding is secured. Clarke asked whether funders have considered supporting applicants during the pre-application phase to facilitate authentic engagement, akin to a supported letter-of-intent process. Stout responded that some SAMHSA grants—particularly those related to substance misuse prevention—have built-in planning periods, often used to review data and establish local partnerships. She added that during the early phase of the Strategic Prevention Framework State Incentive Grants, states convened epidemiological workgroups to analyze data and prioritize areas for action before sub-awarding funds to communities. While not a perfect model, Stout offered this as an example of how planning and community engagement can occur without locking grantees into a fixed proposal at the outset.

Clarke followed up with a concern that even in programs with a formal planning phase, applicants may feel constrained by what they initially proposed. If the community identifies different priorities during the planning phase, she asked, how much flexibility do grantees have to adjust course? Stout acknowledged the tension, but reiterated that in some funding models, communities are not required to pre-select specific issues prior to the planning phase. While the process is not entirely open-ended, she said, there is still room for alignment with evolving community input.

Rozek added that from the funder side, it is important to think flexibly. He described instances where Face the Fight grants were altered midstream in response to implementation challenges or a misalignment with the intended audience. "We could let this play out and say, 'This is a contract and it's going to fail,'" he said. "Or we could develop new KPIs [key performance indicators] and new targets and shift the grant." This sometimes involved additional funding, he noted, but was necessary to ensure the work stayed relevant and impactful. Stressing that flexibility and innovation are key, Rozek emphasized the importance of compensating community members for their time and expertise when asked to contribute and being creative in working within rigid funding structures.

Walsh closed the session by thanking both panels and inviting attendees to continue the discussion throughout the remainder of the workshop.

REFERENCES

Centers for Disease Control and Prevention. (2022). *Suicide prevention resource for action: A compilation of the best available evidence.* https://www.cdc.gov/suicide/pdf/preventionresource.pdf

Crosby, A. E., Han, B., Ortega, L. A., Parks, S. E., & Gfroerer, J. (2011). Suicidal thoughts and behaviors among adults aged ≥18 years—United States, 2008-2009. *Morbidity and Mortality Weekly Report. Surveillance Summaries, 60*(13), 1–22. Centers for Disease Control and Prevention. https://www.cdc.gov/mmwr/preview/mmwrhtml/ss6013a1.htm

Curtin, S. C., & Hedegaard, H. (2019, June). *Suicide rates for females and males by race and ethnicity: United States, 1999 and 2017.* National Center for Health Statistics Health E-Stats. https://www.cdc.gov/nchs/data/hestat/suicide/rates_1999_2017.pdf

Education Development Center. (2025). Community-led suicide prevention online toolkit. https://communitysuicideprevention.org/

Hedegaard, H., Curtin, S. C., & Warner, M. (2020). Increase in suicide mortality in the United States, 1999–2018 (NCHS Data Brief No. 362) National Center for Health Statistics. https://www.cdc.gov/nchs/data/databriefs/db362-h.pdf

National Action Alliance for Suicide Prevention. (2017). *Transforming communities: Key elements for the implementation of comprehensive community-based suicide prevention.* Education Development Center. https://theactionalliance.org/sites/default/files/transformingcommunitiespaper.pdf

Potter, L. B., Powell, K. E., & Kachur, S. P. (1995). Suicide prevention from a public health perspective. *Suicide & Life-Threatening Behavior, 25*(1), 82–91.

Ramchand, R., Senator, B., Davis, J. P., Hawkins, W., Jaycox, L. H., Lejeune, J., Livingston, W. S., Locker, A. R., Trachik, B., & Athey, A. (2025). *Preventing veteran suicide: A landscape analysis of existing programs, their evidence, and what the next generation of programs may look like.* RAND Corporation. https://www.rand.org/pubs/research_reports/RRA3635-1.html

Suicide Prevention Resource Center. (2020a). Comprehensive approach to suicide prevention. https://sprc.org/effective-prevention/comprehensive-approach

___. (2020b). Strategic planning approach to suicide prevention. https://sprc.org/effective-prevention/strategic-planning/

U.S. Department of Health and Human Services. (2024). *National strategy for suicide prevention.* https://www.hhs.gov/sites/default/files/national-strategy-suicide-prevention.pdf

U.S. Department of Veterans Affairs. (2018). *National strategy for preventing veteran suicide.* https://www.mentalhealth.va.gov/suicide_prevention/docs/Office-of-Mental-Health-and-Suicide-Prevention-National-Strategy-for-Preventing-Veterans-Suicide.pdf

___. (2024). *2024 National veteran suicide prevention annual report, part 2 of 2: Report findings.* https://www.mentalhealth.va.gov/docs/data-sheets/2024/2024-Annual-Report-Part-2-of-2_508.pdf

Wisconsin Department of Health and Human Services. (n.d.). *Moving prevention upstream.* https://www.dhs.wisconsin.gov/publications/p02695a.pdf

World Health Organization. (2014). *Preventing suicide: A global imperative.* https://iris.who.int/handle/10665/131056

4

Considerations for Program Evaluation

The next session of the workshop was focused on program evaluation. The session opened with two presentations that established a conceptual basis for broader dialogue in the subsequent moderated panel discussion. Following the panel discussion, the final portion of the session was dedicated to audience Q&A.

This chapter highlights practical strategies and real-world lessons for evaluating suicide prevention programs at the community level. Speakers emphasized the importance of aligning evaluation design with program goals, engaging communities in meaningful ways, and using evaluation data to drive learning, accountability, and improvement.

LESSONS LEARNED AND EXAMPLES FROM THE FIELD

Two speakers shared insights from their long-standing roles in evaluating suicide prevention programs. The first presentation provided an overview of key concepts and decision points in program evaluation design, while the second drew on nearly two decades of experience with a national youth suicide prevention initiative to illustrate lessons learned in practice.

From Program Evaluation to Comprehensive, Community-Based Suicide Prevention Evaluation: Lessons Learned from the Field

Kristen Quinlan (Education Development Center, National Action Alliance for Suicide Prevention) opened her presentation by highlighting her dual roles: providing training and technical assistance to states and communities on evaluation and serving as a representative of the National Action Alliance for Suicide Prevention. In both capacities, she emphasized the importance of integrating evaluation into broader, coordinated, and public health–oriented approaches to suicide prevention.

Quinlan began by acknowledging the major frameworks currently guiding community-based suicide prevention efforts, including the National Strategy for Veteran Suicide Prevention 2018–2028, the 2024 National Strategy for Suicide Prevention, and the accompanying Federal Action Plan. These frameworks share a commitment to upstream and downstream prevention and to comprehensive, coordinated approaches. She emphasized that these same principles should inform how program evaluation is approached.

Quinlan framed logic models as familiar and useful tools for evaluation, referencing Standley's earlier presentation. A typical logic model progresses from inputs and activities to outputs and then short-, intermediate-, and long-term outcomes. In suicide prevention, long-term outcomes often refer to sustained behavior change, infrastructure, and policy development. However, Quinlan noted that many programs are asked to show impact, especially reductions in suicide rates, without regard for the scale or scope of their contribution to the overall prevention effort.

She cautioned against treating evaluation in isolation, particularly for community-based efforts, which do not occur in a vacuum. Rather, these programs often work in synergy with broader community and state-level inputs and assets. "When we evaluate what we are doing," she said, "we can't tell the story in a vacuum either." She stressed the importance of articulating a program's unique contribution while avoiding the temptation to overstate its impact.

For example, a program focused on raising awareness about 988 may play a vital role in a community's overall suicide prevention strategy, but it is not responsible for outcomes related to treatment or crisis intervention. Rather than claim full credit for broader impacts, programs should clearly communicate what they were responsible for. "We want to be real about what we can do," she explained, "and what we're on the hook for."

Quinlan also addressed the limitations of impact measurement at the community level. Suicide is a relatively rare event, and in smaller populations, even minor changes in the number of deaths can lead to dramatic fluctuations in rates. These "small Ns," she noted, can make it difficult to demonstrate stable trends over time and may lead to premature dismissal of effective programs based on incomplete or misleading data. Instead, she argued, the field must move beyond a narrow emphasis on impact and work toward telling a more complete story of progress.

To support this shift, Quinlan introduced a "nested evaluation model" (see Figure 4-1), in which individual program evaluations are situated

FIGURE 4-1 Nested evaluation model for suicide prevention.
SOURCE: Presentation by Kristen Quinlan on April 29, 2025.

within a broader framework of shared state and/or community inputs and goals. She explained that using common logic models and shared metrics allows diverse programs to contribute to a collective evaluation strategy that is better able to assess short-, intermediate-, and long-term outcomes.

Quinlan offered the Colorado National Collaborative as a real-world example of this approach. The initiative was sparked by a meeting of national, state, and local suicide prevention leaders who asked what might happen if high-risk counties implemented upstream and downstream prevention activities simultaneously, rather than through uncoordinated one-off efforts.

Colorado was selected for its strong infrastructure and existing Office of Suicide Prevention. Six high-risk counties with diverse geographic, demographic, and socioeconomic profiles were chosen. Each county agreed to focus on six core suicide prevention priorities, but they were given the freedom to pursue these goals in ways that made sense for their communities. While this variation presented challenges for evaluation, it reflected the need for local flexibility. As long as counties could document their outputs and address shared metrics related to the six pillars—such as connectedness and economic support—the effort could be evaluated through a unified, albeit adaptable, framework. Quinlan added that the Colorado initiative was in its fifth year of funding, and while full evaluation results were still pending, the project exemplified how aligned implementation and evaluation strategies can support community-based prevention at scale.

Looking ahead, she previewed an initiative led by the National Action Alliance for Suicide Prevention to develop a national monitoring and evaluation strategy aligned with the National Strategy for Suicide Prevention. Still in its early stages, the effort aims to help states, tribes, jurisdictions, and communities better align their evaluation efforts with national priorities. The goal is to enable communities to "plug into" shared templates and logic models to clearly articulate their contributions—even if those contributions address only a portion of the national strategy. Through common core metrics and shared frameworks, the evaluation conversation can shift away from the binary of "strategy or impact," toward a more nuanced understanding of short-, intermediate-, and long-term progress.

In the final portion of her talk, Quinlan focused on the importance of engaging communities in the evaluation process. As an evaluation trainer, she emphasized the goal of building local capacity so that evaluation efforts can be sustained after external support ends. This requires a participatory approach, in which community stakeholders are meaningfully involved in every stage of the evaluation.

Quinlan shared several principles for participatory evaluation, which incorporates invested parties as leaders in all aspects of the evaluation (see

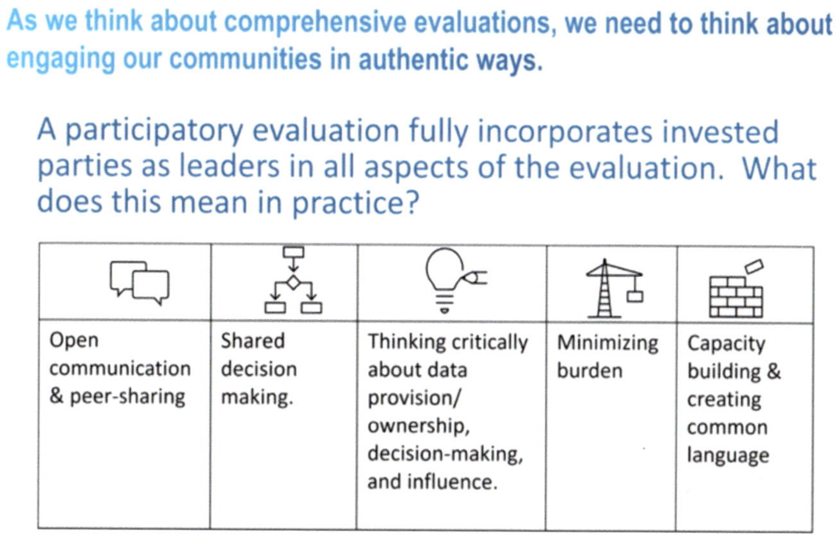

As we think about comprehensive evaluations, we need to think about engaging our communities in authentic ways.

A participatory evaluation fully incorporates invested parties as leaders in all aspects of the evaluation. What does this mean in practice?

Open communication & peer-sharing	Shared decision making.	Thinking critically about data provision/ ownership, decision-making, and influence.	Minimizing burden	Capacity building & creating common language

FIGURE 4-2 Principles of participatory evaluation in community-based suicide prevention.
SOURCE: Presentation by Kristen Quinlan on April 29, 2025.

Figure 4-2), including the use of common language, minimizing community burden, encouraging peer learning, and promoting shared decision-making. She called attention to the issue of data ownership and feedback, noting that communities are often tasked with providing data without receiving sufficient access to or benefit from the results. As an example, she described a stakeholder mapping exercise conducted in Colorado to examine who collects, owns, and uses data. The exercise revealed a pattern in which certain actors bore most of the data collection burden while receiving little in return. "If we are going to collect it," she concluded, "we need to be sure we are feeding the information back."

Multi-Site Community-Based Suicide Prevention Program Evaluation: An Example from the Field

Christine Walrath (ICF) delivered a comprehensive presentation on the evaluation of the Garrett Lee Smith (GLS) Suicide Prevention Program, detailing its evolution, challenges, and insights from nearly two decades of implementation. She began by setting the context for the GLS program, which funds state, tribal, and campus grantees to implement suicide prevention efforts for youth and young adults. Over time, the evaluation strategy has transitioned from focusing primarily on implementation to examining outcomes more rigorously.

Walrath noted that evaluation efforts began at the launch of the program, and evaluation and data-driven decision making were part of the requirements in the Garrett Lee Smith Memorial Act. The act required grantees to participate in evaluation efforts, so there were local and national evaluation elements. The evaluation requirements created an environment and culture that had evaluation embedded in program decision making and that has continued throughout life of grant programs locally and nationally. Over time, the approach evolved to include targeted studies on the effectiveness of the program, more sophisticated statistical modeling, and dissemination of findings in academic publications and summary briefs.

A key theme of Walrath's presentation was the inherent complexity in evaluating a large federal program that funds diverse interventions across a range of sites. These differences span geographic contexts, population demographics, implementation capacity, and intervention models. To respond to this complexity, the evaluation team adopted a mixed-methods, multilevel approach, including both quantitative and qualitative data collection and analysis. This approach allowed them to understand not only what outcomes were achieved, but how and under what conditions they were achieved.

She emphasized the importance of using data to tell a compelling story—one that speaks to both statistical outcomes and human experiences. For example, she presented findings showing statistically significant declines in suicide attempts among youth served by GLS grantees compared to control groups and increases in knowledge and awareness among gatekeepers trained by the program. She also referenced qualitative insights that provided richer understanding of how interventions were experienced by participants.

One key lesson from the GLS evaluation, Walrath noted, was the value of designing evaluation methods that are flexible enough to adapt to evolving program needs while maintaining scientific rigor. This required building strong relationships with grantees and technical assistance providers, so that data collection efforts were feasible and aligned with real-world implementation. It also meant carefully balancing the need for standardization (to allow for cross-site comparisons) with responsiveness to the unique features of each grantee site.

Walrath shared examples of how findings from the evaluation have informed both policy and practice. For instance, the results helped make the case for sustained and increased funding for suicide prevention programs and shaped the development of new tools and resources to support grantees. She also highlighted the use of dashboards and other visual tools to communicate evaluation findings to diverse audiences, including policymakers, program staff, and community members.

In closing, Walrath reflected on the broader implications of the GLS evaluation for suicide prevention and public health more generally. She stressed the need for continued investment in evaluation infrastructure, capacity-building among grantees, and the use of data not just for accountability, but for learning and continuous improvement. "Evaluation," she noted, "should not be an afterthought. It should be built into the program from the start."

PANEL DISCUSSION AND AUDIENCE Q&A

Following the two presentations on program evaluation, the presenters were joined by individuals who had given the presentations summarized in Chapter 2: Mary Cwik (Johns Hopkins University), Novalene Alsenay Goklish (Johns Hopkins University), Brandi Jancaitis (Virginia Department of Veterans Services), Richard McKeon (Substance Abuse and Mental Health Services Administration), and David Rozek (University of Texas Health Science Center at San Antonio), along with Tanha Patel (Centers for Disease Control and Prevention Foundation), for a moderated panel discussion to reflect on practical strategies, challenges, and lessons learned related to evaluating suicide prevention programs and communicating results to diverse audiences. Diana Clarke (American Psychiatric Association; member, workshop planning committee) served as the moderator for this discussion. Panelists responded to guiding questions on the following topics: evolution of program design and administration based on evaluation findings, best practices for balancing evaluation across multiple levels, using intermediate indicators to track progress toward suicide prevention goals, and grantee involvement in evaluation and building and sustaining capacity over time.

Evolution of Program Design and Administration Based on Evaluation Findings

Clarke began the discussion by asking panel members to reflect on how program design and administration has evolved over time passed on evaluation findings and lessons learned. Quinlan emphasized the growing role of participatory action approaches and the need to invest in community-based infrastructure for data collection. She shared an example of a county-level youth program that initially relied on school-based surveys but faced objections from parents. In response, the team pivoted to key informant interviews and focus groups with youth. When those results were shared, community members asked how to obtain a more representative sample, prompting further adaptation. Quinlan noted that this cycle of feedback and adjustment exemplifies the value of participatory approaches in ensuring that communities have the information that they need to grow and sustain their prevention efforts.

Patel described an initiative supporting veteran-serving organizations that evolved significantly over seven years of implementation. Early in the program, technical assistance providers discovered that many of the participating organizations had limited staff and capacity for evaluation. Tools were developed to support them, but each year those tools had to be adapted based on where organizations were in their readiness. Eventually, a toolkit was created to support organizations beyond the initial grantee group, incorporating input from participants in the program's final two years. Patel underscored the importance of engaging participants to ensure that the tools were relevant, understandable, and aligned with their actual needs, emphasizing that building this capacity takes time and sustained investment.

Cwik shared that her team's evaluation findings also prompted a significant shift in their programming approach. Initially, they had focused on adapting existing programs for use in tribal communities, but evaluations showed that while these programs were often strong in some areas, they were not always a good cultural fit. In response, the team shifted toward creating innovative programs from the ground up with guidance from tribal Elders to ensure cultural alignment and community ownership.

McKeon described several ways in which data collected through program evaluation influenced efforts to refine and adjust funding priorities under the GLS grant program. One area of focus, he noted, was determining where grantees were directing their suicide prevention efforts. Evaluation data revealed that the vast majority of grantees were implementing school-based suicide prevention activities. While this focus was valuable—given that schools provide a universal access point for reaching youth—McKeon noted that other high-risk populations were receiving less attention. "We were getting occasional really good grantee work on juvenile justice or foster care," he said, "but not as much as I would have liked." Although some projects addressed youth in mental health settings, there were very few focused on youth involved in the juvenile justice or child welfare systems—despite their elevated suicide risk. McKeon referenced a study from Utah that found 60% of youth who died by suicide had previous involvement in the juvenile justice system. The question became whether similar patterns existed in other states, and what more could be done to encourage targeted interventions for these populations.

To support a potential shift, McKeon's team asked the Suicide Prevention Research Center to conduct an analysis of suicide prevention efforts within juvenile justice and foster care systems. The hope was to generate guidance and recommendations that could spur increased engagement by states and tribes with these high-risk populations. While some grantees responded and pursued work in these areas, McKeon acknowledged that uptake was limited, in part due to constraints in statutory language governing the grant program. Legal and policy restrictions also created barriers to directly funding suicide prevention in some justice settings, such as jails. He noted there was a little more flexibility with detention centers, but it was mostly limited to training staff, not providing services. Despite the limitations, McKeon emphasized that this was a data-driven effort to evolve the program in response to identified gaps. The evaluation revealed where needs existed, and while the changes were only partially successful, they reflected an intentional effort to align funding priorities with the goal of reaching higher-risk youth.

Clarke summarized a key theme across the examples: the need for both programs and funders to evolve together. Meaningful change is most likely when community capacity-building is coupled with program flexibility and responsiveness to evaluation.

Best Practices for Balancing Evaluation Across Multiple Levels

Clarke next asked panelists to identify best practices for balancing evaluation across multiple levels—individual grantees, clusters of similar grantees, and overarching program efforts. Walrath emphasized the importance of planning to create data collection strategies that serve multiple purposes. Rather than thinking of it as a matter of balance, she suggested that evaluation designers should identify essential indicators upfront that can be useful at local, cluster, and national levels. With this kind of strategic forethought, programs can avoid duplicative data collection and ensure that data gathered serve a range of evaluation needs.

Jancaitis offered lessons from her team's work in Virginia, noting that they are still actively learning how to categorize grantees in ways that allow for meaningful aggregation and storytelling. She described grantees ranging from organizations providing direct peer counseling to others focused on gatekeeper training, emphasizing the need to develop tailored subsets of measures for different types of interventions. Jancaitis acknowledged that when programs move quickly to get funding into communities, as was the case for her team, data strategies may be less developed initially. However, she stressed the value of learning alongside grantees and adapting over time—particularly when grantees highlight that certain data points are not useful or suggest better ways to frame findings. For example, when talking to legislators, reframing impact in terms of household effects rather than individual veterans allowed for broader, more meaningful storytelling.

Jancaitis also shared a challenge they encountered in using clinical language, such as the term "safety plan." While common in provider settings, she noted that this language sometimes triggered concern among veterans, who associated it with hospitalization and loss of rights. This made engagement difficult. She stressed the importance of tailoring terminology to the cultural and lived experience of the community being served.

Rozek underscored the importance of transparency and communication around evaluation metrics. He noted that when grantees are asked to report data without understanding its purpose, it can feel arbitrary or burdensome. To address this, his team works collaboratively with grantees to explain why specific data elements are requested and whether they are feasible to collect. If a data point would require an excessive time investment, Rozek said, they reconsider whether it is truly essential. He emphasized that data should be actionable for both the funder and the grantee, and that ongoing conversations are key to ensuring mutual understanding and relevance.

Patel added a perspective from her previous role working on National Institutes of Health–funded multi-site programs. She described how funder guidance on performance measures, combined with opportunities for evaluators to connect in peer groups, helped foster shared learning and collaboration. These informal workgroups allowed evaluators to explore common interests—such as implementation or outcome evaluations—and build a community of practice that extended beyond the life of the grant. Patel emphasized that these evaluator-to-evaluator connections strengthened the evaluation process and helped align efforts across sites.

Clarke closed the discussion by affirming the importance of participatory evaluation approaches. She emphasized that evaluation is most effective when it is not imposed on organizations but co-created with them—an insight echoed throughout the conversation.

Using Intermediate Indicators to Track Progress Toward Suicide Prevention Goals

Clarke invited panelists to discuss best practices for identifying and using intermediate indicators in program evaluation. Noting that many presentations had touched on this theme, she asked how programs should approach the development and use of such indicators. Cwik responded by emphasizing the importance of grounding evaluation efforts in a logic model or theory of change. These models, she explained, help programs articulate what they expect their interventions to impact and how those effects might ultimately reduce suicide risk. "Sometimes you have to take a guess," she acknowledged, adding that the path to suicide prevention is not always linear or obvious. Cwik offered the New Hope program as an example. While the ultimate goal is to reduce suicide and suicide deaths, hypothesized intermediate outcomes include reduced depressive symptoms, decreased suicidal ideation, and increased reasons for hope. Identifying the most appropriate indicators may require returning to relevant scientific literature, consulting with clinicians and community members, and conducting small pilot tests that track multiple potential outcomes to see which ones are most responsive to the intervention.

Quinlan added that early engagement with community stakeholders and other invested parties is essential. These groups can help clarify what they care about, what they want to learn from the evaluation, and where they expect to see change. "There's nothing more disappointing than to build an evaluation not built on what the community wants to know," she said. Asking the right questions from the outset and grounding evaluation in what the community values can help identify meaningful intermediate outcomes.

Walrath emphasized that logic models and theories of change should not be viewed as static documents. Rather, they should be dynamic—revisited and refined over time as programs learn more about their effects. Programs may initially identify a "best guess" about short-, intermediate-, and long-term outcomes, but these assumptions should be adjusted as new evidence becomes available.

Quinlan added that traditional logic model formats do not always resonate with all communities. Linear models, she noted, may not reflect how certain cultural groups conceptualize change. She encouraged funders and evaluators to consider alternative approaches to logic modeling, such as using visual metaphors like canoes or circles. These adaptations can better align with community values and worldviews while still providing a roadmap for evaluation. Returning to the broader theme of community engagement and inclusive evaluation, Quinlan described a past SAMHSA program called Service to Science. The initiative paired evaluators with grassroots organizations to help translate their work into the language of funders and evaluation. She stated that there is a lot of great practice-to-evidence work occurring, but these efforts often do not speak the language of the funder. Service to Science helped bridge this gap by providing training and support in evaluation while also encouraging funders to expand their definitions of acceptable evidence. Rather than prioritizing only randomized controlled trials, Quinlan said, the program encouraged exploration of other methodologically sound approaches that better captured different ways of knowing.

Clarke commented that evaluators should also consider how they define positive versus negative outcomes. Drawing from her experience as a clinical researcher, she cautioned that metrics traditionally viewed as negative—such as increased hospitalizations—may, in some contexts, reflect positive developments. For example, if a suicide prevention program led to more individuals seeking care at hospitals or emergency departments, that may indicate greater willingness to reach out for help rather than an increase in crisis events. The perception of outcomes can shape interpretation of program impact, she noted. She encouraged evaluators to reflect critically on how success is defined and measured, particularly in areas as complex as suicide prevention.

Grantee Involvement in Evaluation and Building and Sustaining Capacity Over Time

The next question posed by Clarke was "What role should grantees play in the evaluation and what support do they need to do it well and to sustain it over time?" Rozek stressed the importance of understanding the data that grantees are already collecting. In one instance, he noted, the funder team was prepared to introduce a standard set of evaluation metrics when a simple question—"What else are you already collecting?"—revealed that the grantee had already amassed a rich set of tailored data. "Some of these organizations have amazing, very rich data," Rozek said, "and sometimes even better measures than what we ask from common data elements because they are tailored to the program." In some cases, programs had already conducted psychometric assessments or developed custom outcome measures to meet the needs of their communities. Rozek emphasized that if evaluation is approached as a true collaboration—where funders are willing to listen, share reasoning behind requests, and negotiate when appropriate—it can be mutually beneficial. Importantly, he added, grantees often possess valuable insights about what works and why, but those insights may be overlooked unless explicitly invited into the conversation.

Jancaitis echoed the need for funders to approach evaluation as a true collaboration and to be responsive to grantee feedback. She offered examples from her own work in which grantees explained why their sample sizes were small or why additional time was needed to build trust and reach vulnerable populations. In one case, a peer support grantee shared that it could take six months before someone was even willing to talk. Funders, she emphasized, should consider the human realities behind the data and buffer grantees from excessive burden whenever possible. She noted that flexibility in implementation requirements—such as when and how screening is conducted—can help align evaluation with real-world program delivery.

Within the GLS program, Walrath shared, grantees were supported by a team that included a grant project officer, a technical assistance provider, and an evaluation support person. This wraparound support helped grantees integrate evaluation into their existing workflows, regardless of the specific setting or strategy being implemented. She referred to these support roles as "program partners" who could adapt evaluation approaches to fit the grantee's context and make implementation as seamless as possible.

Patel highlighted two critical needs for supporting grantee participation in evaluation: funding and time. Without dedicated evaluation resources and time to plan and execute evaluation activities across the program life cycle, she cautioned, efforts are likely to be limited to basic reporting. "To really get to the stories of what's meaningful," she said, "it will take time and money." Clarke then asked for specifics on the type of training provided to build grantee capacity to lead evaluation, in response to which Patel added that her program is fundamentally designed to provide training, technical assistance, and capacity-building support for evaluation. Organizations participate in a structured cohort for approximately 8 to 12 months, during which they receive both group-based instruction and individualized technical assistance. "We don't expect our grantees to come in with evaluation knowledge," Patel said. "If they know the bare bones—'Hey, I need to do evaluation; my funder is asking me to do this'—that's where we get them." Participants are introduced to core concepts of evaluation and guided through the process of building an evaluation plan for one suicide prevention program. The plan is structured so that it can be replicated across other programs within the organization, with the goal of establishing lasting internal capacity for evaluation.

Quinlan added that in some cases, the first step is simply making the case for why evaluation is needed at all. She recalled a conversation with a community pastor who declined to engage in evaluation training, saying, "I'm busy putting out fires." In such cases, she said, it is essential to show how evaluation can help sustain the program and communicate its impact to funders, stakeholders, and the broader community. "To be able to lay the foundation that it's even needed is sometimes where you need to start," she noted.

These reflections underscored that building evaluation capacity is not only a technical challenge, but also a relational and motivational one. For grantees to lead evaluation effectively, they must be given not only tools and training, but also a clear understanding of the value and purpose of evaluation within their specific context.

Audience Q&A

The session concluded with a robust audience discussion, both in-person and online, that explored issues of data infrastructure, culturally responsive evaluation, and the importance of clear and inclusive assessment practices, particularly in work with tribal and veteran communities.

Exploring Federated Data Systems and Common Data Elements

A member of the virtual audience asked about the potential to develop federated learning models or data sharing platforms that preserve individual privacy while enabling linkage across multiple programs and organizations.

Walrath shared that an ongoing evaluation of the 988 and behavioral health crisis continuum initiative includes a conceptual exploration of cross-linked data environments at the state level. Though still aspirational, she noted that the evaluation is looking at ways to connect data across crisis response systems and ultimately link to the National Death Index. Crosby added that some preliminary work has occurred in states using the National Violent Death Reporting System to link death data with correctional or other state-level administrative records. These efforts remain limited to the state level, he noted, as personally identifiable information typically falls under state authority. Rozek shared an example from Face the Fight, which is partnering with the Institute for Veterans and Military Families at Syracuse University. This grantee is working with coalition partners to gather social determinants of health data across veteran-serving organizations using common data elements. Rozek noted that the long-term goal is to establish data sharing agreements—while protecting privacy—that would enable pooled, de-identified data to be analyzed at scale. However, he emphasized that funder support is essential for standardizing data collection and building a shared repository of usable, accessible information.

Clarke pointed out that research studies funded by the National Institute of Mental Health and other federal agencies already require data deposition into repositories, making those data available for cross-study analysis. She reiterated the importance of common data elements for meaningful comparison across studies and highlighted the challenges of cross-walking between different tools without a shared standard—particularly when large samples are needed. McKeon underscored that data linkage, in addition to common data elements, is critical. He referenced the Utah youth suicide study as a powerful example, where public records were used to trace contact across youth-serving systems. The study revealed that 60 percent of youth who died by suicide in Utah had prior involvement with the juvenile justice system—higher than contact with the mental health system. That kind of trajectory mapping, he said, offers insight into pathways for intervention. While Utah has since replicated and expanded the study, McKeon noted that few others have followed suit. He added that SAMHSA's evaluation of behavioral crisis services, including the 988 platform, is one of the most ambitious of its kind, but navigating the balance between standardization and customization remains a persistent challenge.

Incorporating Cultural Values into Evaluation and Data Sharing with Tribal Communities

Another member of the virtual audience asked how evaluation tools used in suicide prevention incorporate culturally specific values, beliefs, and protective factors unique to tribal communities, and what culturally appropriate methods of data sharing have proven most effective in fostering trust, reciprocity, and inter-tribal learning. Cwik shared that her team routinely adapts standardized measures based on tribal community input. Community members are invited to review survey tools for face validity, language clarity, and cultural fit. Edits may be made to existing questions or new questions added to reflect local priorities. In addition to modifying standardized tools, the team incorporates qualitative approaches to surface risk and protective factors not captured by traditional instruments. These might include measures of cultural connectedness, experiences of historical trauma, or other culturally salient constructs.

Goklish expanded on Cwik's response by explaining how evaluation tools are reviewed through a community advisory board to ensure cultural appropriateness. Community members, including those not typically involved in research, offer feedback to ensure language is respectful, relevant, and unlikely to offend. Goklish emphasized the importance of staff comfort as well—if frontline staff are uneasy administering an evaluation, it compromises both the data quality and the trust between programs and participants. In some cases, tools must be translated into Apache, requiring close attention to nuance, meaning, and cultural context to avoid miscommunication.

Clarke followed up with a question directed to Jancaitis about tailoring assessment tools for the military and veteran populations. Jancaitis stressed the need for alignment in how military and veteran status is defined and captured. Different programs use different definitions—for example, VA-eligible veterans versus anyone who has served in the military with any discharge status—and this can create challenges for both service delivery and cross-program referrals. She urged that data systems include not just information on service members and veterans, but also their families. "They are a key path to that service member or veteran that may not have otherwise engaged," she said. Capturing data on partners, loved ones, and children is essential to serving the full ecosystem of support that surrounds veterans.

Clarke closed the session by thanking the presenters and panelists for the wide-ranging discussion and emphasized the need to continue conversations around data infrastructure, cultural responsiveness, and community-informed evaluation approaches.

5

Communicating Program Results

After the session focused on program evaluation, the workshop turned to the topic of communicating program results. The session opened with two presentations that established a conceptual basis for broader dialogue in the subsequent moderated panel discussion. Following the panel discussion, the final portion of the session was dedicated to an audience Q&A.

This chapter offers guidance for developing communication strategies that amplify program impact and promote engagement. Effective communication of program results requires intentional strategy, audience engagement, and thoughtful message design. Drawing on insights from behavioral science and suicide prevention practice, this chapter outlines best practices for dissemination—including audience tailoring, data storytelling, visual design, and real-time adaptation—and presents examples of how communication can support impact, build coalitions, and inform public dialogue.

STRATEGIC COMMUNICATION AND DATA STORYTELLING

The foundational presentations in this session explored strategic approaches to communicating program results. Speakers focused on tailoring communications to particular audiences and using data storytelling to convey impact in ways that are clear, compelling, and meaningful to diverse stakeholders.

Best Processes for Strategic Communication of Program Results

Jeff Niederdeppe (Cornell University) began by suggesting it is more appropriate to think in terms of best *processes*, rather than best *practices*, as there is no one-size-fits-all approach to effective communication and dissemination. However, he explained, a set of helpful questions and frameworks can guide efforts. Because communication and dissemination activities are often carried out under resource constraints, he stressed the importance of having a clear strategy to maximize impact. Niederdeppe urged participants to bring the same level of thought and planning to communication and dissemination that is typically applied to program implementation and evaluation, emphasizing that some of the same principles and concepts apply across both domains.

Niederdeppe identified a set of key strategic questions that should guide communication and dissemination efforts:

1. Why communicate program results?
2. How should program results be communicated?
   - To whom to say it?
   - What to say?
   - When to say it?
   - Where to say it (via what channels)?
   - How to say it (e.g., stories, evidence, figures, statistics)?
3. Is there potential for unintended negative consequences?

Put more succinctly, in communication and dissemination, the foundational questions are who, what, when, where, why, how, and with what potential risk. Of these, he noted, *why* is the most important question—why are we disseminating program results? What is the goal? What is the purpose of these dissemination efforts? He followed up these questions by pointing to the complexity of behavioral, institutional, and policy change processes, which are rarely linear.

To illustrate this complexity, Niederdeppe presented two conceptual models: the COM-B model of planning behavioral interventions and a typical policy process logic model (see Figure 5-1). He emphasized the circular nature of the two models, with various overlapping and intervening factors that may or may not coalesce to create momentum for change. Understanding which pieces must coalesce for change to happen is essential, he said, for determining how and when evidence might inform practice and policy. One pathway is agenda-setting—identifying a topic, program, or policy as important and worthy of attention. Another pathway, Niderdeppe continued, is direct advocacy or persuasion: convincing key audiences that an intervention should be implemented or that an issue should be reframed.

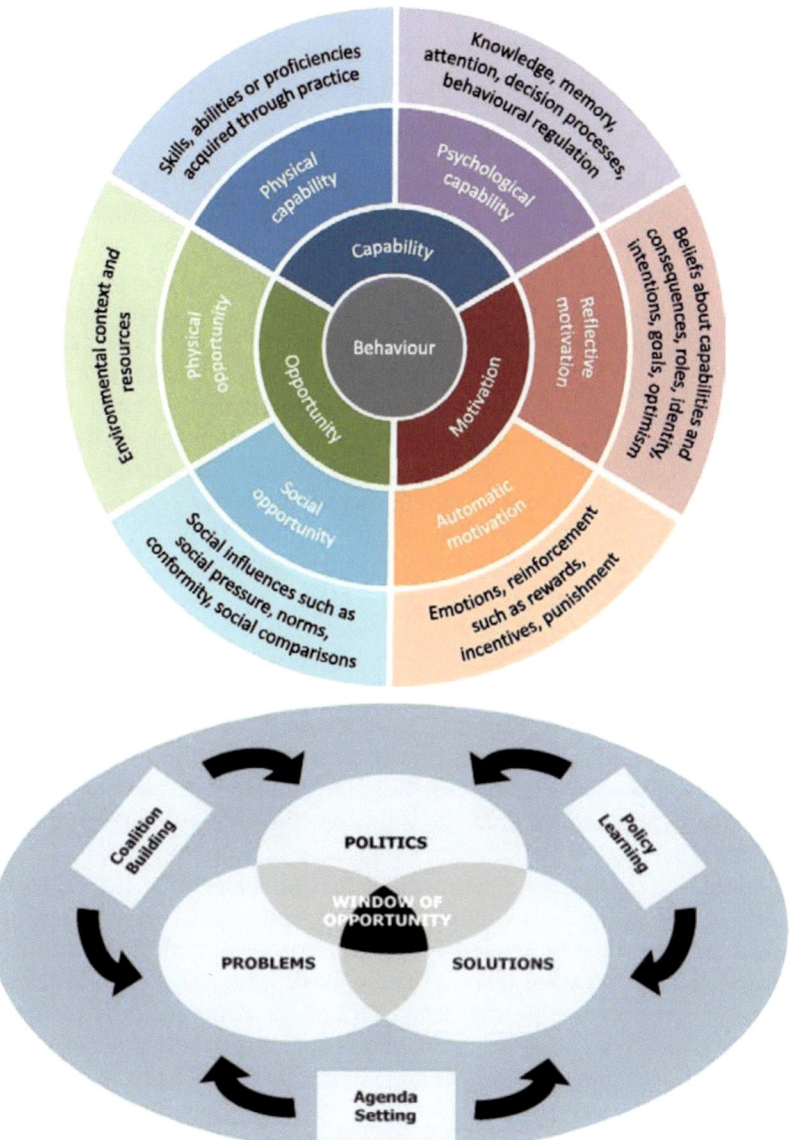

FIGURE 5-1 The COM-B model of planning behavioral interventions and a "typical" logic model of the policy process.
SOURCES: Presented by Jeff Niederdeppe on April 29, 2025. The COM-B model (top) is reprinted from McDonagh and colleagues (2018) under a Creative Commons Attribution 4.0 International License (http://creativecommons.org/licenses/by/4.0/). The Population Reference Bureau Policy Process: A Theoretical Framework (bottom) is reprinted with permission from Population Reference Bureau (2009).

A third pathway involves mobilizing constituencies, building coalitions, and bringing together stakeholders with shared interests to collaborate on an issue. These strategies are not mutually exclusive, but each requires resources.

Each of these pathways suggests a different set of behaviors and foci, Niederdeppe observed, underscoring the need for a clearly articulated goal and a corresponding theory of change to guide dissemination decisions. If the goal is agenda-setting, Niederdeppe explained, the strategy might involve maximizing community exposure to a topic, because people would see the topic being raised repeatedly as important. If the goal is persuasion, attention must be given to identifying the specific actors to be persuaded, whether they are decision makers, knowledge brokers, or other intermediaries. Reframing an issue toward a more public health community-based approach may require crafting messages that align with shared values and invite audiences to see the issue the same way. Reflecting on the day's emphasis on a comprehensive public health approach to suicide prevention, Niederdeppe added that while this framing is widely used among researchers and practitioners, it may not resonate as strongly with general policymakers or lay audiences.

If the goal is coalition-building, Niederdeppe continued, it is necessary to determine which organizations and individuals to engage; engagement may need to extend beyond stakeholders focused on suicide prevention for veterans or military personnel, and include those who care about some broader community-based change ideas central to a public health approach, such as workforce development or building connections between people.

Niederdeppe underscored the importance of identifying the intended audience once the "why" is clear, as decades of communication, and dissemination research have demonstrated that understanding the values and beliefs of the audience is central to crafting messages that will resonate. Here, decisions must be made—is the focus on communicating with institutional decision makers? If so, is the emphasis on trying to persuade those who opposed previous policies or programs, or is the purpose to instead mobilize those who already are inclined to support these policies or programs? Or is the aim to target the general public to build pressure from the ground up? Is the purpose to persuade the public that an issue is important, or is the purpose to mobilize those already affected? Niederdeppe followed up these questions by highlighting that scholarly communities are key actors in a broader dissemination and communication strategy.

The next step is to determine what should be said, Niederdeppe noted, cautioning against the common practice of disseminating findings as new evidence is developed, expecting that exposure alone will lead to change. Instead, he advised starting from the end goal, such as promoting a program or changing policy, and then working backward to understand who the audience is—what are their values and beliefs and how might those drive their support for or opposition to policies or programs (see Figure 5-2). For example, Niederdeppe explained, a decision maker who is trying to decide whether to allocate funding for a suicide prevention program focused on community-level change for veterans might be most persuaded by evidence of improving social connections. For another decision maker, evidence of economic development for veterans, or the overall health impact (suicides prevented, number of people who seek help) might be more persuasive; others might be most concerned about return on investment or political feasibility. Understanding what drives support for or opposition to these policies or programs, he reiterated, is central to determining what messages are likely to resonate with the audience. From there, the process continues by working backward to determine whether new evidence connects directly with the intended audience's values, or if combining it with well-established existing bodies of scientific knowledge or previous experiential or institutional knowledge about how political and program implementation processes will be more effective.

The timing of dissemination is also critical, Niederdeppe noted. The process of policy and program change and implementation is non-linear,

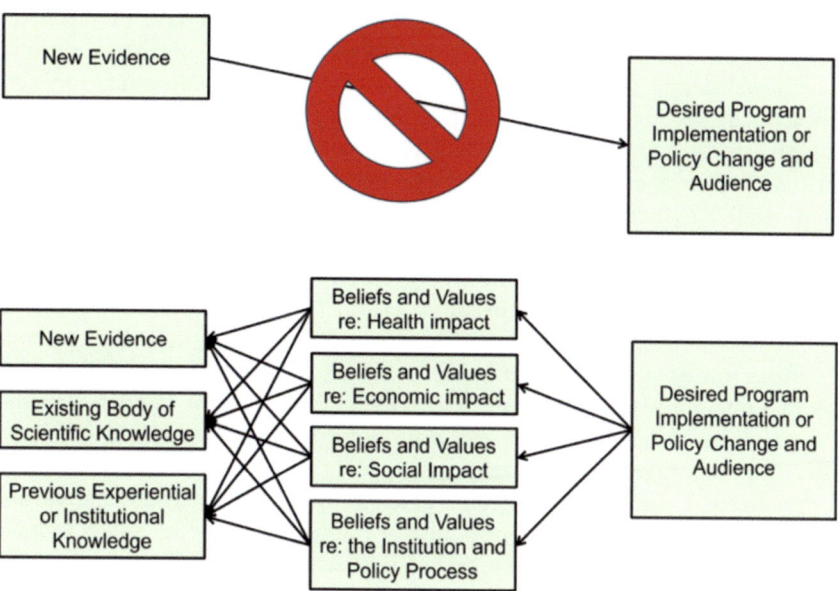

FIGURE 5-2 Think about the desired outcome and work backward to develop communication strategies.
SOURCE: Presented by Jeff Niederdeppe on April 29, 2025.

and different audiences operate on different time horizons that are important to them. Echoing earlier comments from Yanovitzky, he emphasized that it is fundamental to consider a communication strategy from the very beginning, because it is unlikely that critical audiences will need the information at the very moment evidence or results are published or reported. For example, institutional decision makers will not wait for evidence to come by and then make a decision, they are more likely to seek out relevant findings when a policy window opens or a political opportunity arises. Researchers must be ready, Niederdeppe urged, to engage at those moments. Similarly, public interest may depend on personal experience or news relevance, while practice communities often need guidance long before peer-reviewed results are available. On the other hand, he noted, scholarly audiences may require traditional publication but can influence official guidance and professional norms.

Next, Niederdeppe touched upon dissemination channels. The important questions here, he stated, are where is your audience? Where are they engaging with information? What channels resonate with and reach those audiences? Depending on the answers to these questions, relevant channels may include social media, traditional media, community gatherings, or peer-reviewed literature. He cautioned against jumping to social media platforms and engaging influencers without understanding whether such platforms align with the intended audience's habits and preferences. What might work for one audience may be ineffective for another audience.

Niederdeppe went on to highlight the value of communication science for dissemination decisions. Research in this field can help determine whether to use storytelling, anecdotes, emotional appeals, data-driven arguments, or direct engagement with opposition. There is a robust body of work that may help inform decision making, but researchers must engage with the work to make use of it effectively.

Finally, Niederdeppe emphasized the importance of considering potential unintentional negative consequences of dissemination efforts. While it is impossible to anticipate all possible outcomes once information enters a complex information ecosystem, some risks are well documented and should be factored into early planning. He suggested keeping in mind the medical principle of "do no harm" and pointing to the Werther effect—the risk of suicide contagion following publicity of a suicide. Other risks include stigmatization, message co-option, or framing that emphasizes individual responsibility rather than a community or public health model. Niederdeppe closed his presentation by cautioning that disseminating results very publicly can run the risk of catalyzing oppositional forces when a subtler or more focused dissemination strategy with decision makers that does not bring in media attention may have a better chance effecting change under the radar and avoid catalyzing oppositional forces.

Data Storytelling: Best Practices for Communicating Impact

Corbin Standley (American Foundation for Suicide Prevention [AFSP]) opened his presentation by framing data storytelling, which combines data, visuals (such graphs, charts, illustrations), and narratives (such as stories about the program and about those impacted), as an approach that helps data come alive and inspire action. He then laid out three steps for effective storytelling:

1. Knowing the audience. Audience-specific data communication ensures the message is clear, relevant, and impactful.
2. Finding the story. Knowing what the data are saying will help develop a meaningful narrative that is insightful for the audience.
3. Visualizing the impact. Displaying data with the right visuals to ensure the story is communicated clearly and interpreted correctly.

In terms of knowing the audience, Standley said, "I always come back to the evaluator's motto of 'it depends'—how you're communicating depends on who your audience is." The approach to communication should vary depending on who the audience is, what they need, and what response is desired. He suggested considering two guiding questions:

1. What do you want the audience to think, feel, or do as a result of encountering the data story, findings, or results?
2. What does the audience need to know to get there?

He then outlined how this approach could be applied across four key audiences:

1. **Researchers and academia.**
   Desired response: View the findings as credible and as a meaningful contribution to the scholarly discourse.
   What they need to know: Is the data valid and reliable, and adding to the body of knowledge?
2. **Funders or donors.**
   Desired response: Continued or increased support for the programs or interventions.
   What they need to know: How has their investment made—or how will it make—a difference?
3. **Policymakers and staffers.**
   Desired response: Take a legislative or policy action.
   What they need to know: How did or will this affect the constituents in my district?

4. **Community members.**
   Desired response: View the findings as relevant and trustworthy and be motivated to engage.
   What they need to know: How does it affect me, my family, and my community?

To find the story in data, Standley explained, he tends to think about a storytelling structure as a roller coaster, with the storytelling elements taught in middle and high school—rising action, falling action, and conclusion—adapted to a set of five elements and corresponding questions that can help frame findings in a way that resonates with different audiences:

1. **Context:** Why does this matter?
2. **Characters:** Who is impacted by the data and who are the characters in the story?
3. **Climb:** What did the program or intervention do?
4. **Consequence:** What are the findings?
5. **Conclusion:** What does it mean? What should people do as a result? What action are we hoping takes place as a result of these program findings?

To illustrate this approach, Standley shared the development and early evaluation findings from the ASFP program *L.E.T.S. Save Lives*, an introductory suicide program designed by and for Black and African American communities that was launched in February 2024 (see Figure 5-3). The context was that suicide rates have been increasing in Black and African American communities for several years. Standley highlighted Keon Lewis as one of the key characters of this story. Lewis, a college student at the time, was inspired to act as a result of friends losing loved ones to suicide. He joined a local chapter of AFSP and later approached the national office with the goal to develop a program specifically for Black and African American communities. In response ASFP put together an advisory committee of people with lived experience, scholars, researchers, and experts from Black and African American communities to co-develop the *L.E.T.S. Save Lives* program, as well as the evaluation—the climb.

Continuing, Standley shared the consequence—or evaluation findings showed early signs of impact, with over 2,000 people reached, 95 percent of participants reporting they feel comfortable supporting a loved one who may be struggling, and a 20 percent increase in participant likelihood to reach out for support for themselves or others. The conclusion, Standley shared, is that a follow-up survey found 60 percent of participants had reached out to someone that they were concerned about within two months after attending the program. "Conversations are happening that weren't before," he noted. As part of the next phase, Lewis is partnering with AFSP

COMMUNICATING PROGRAM RESULTS   91

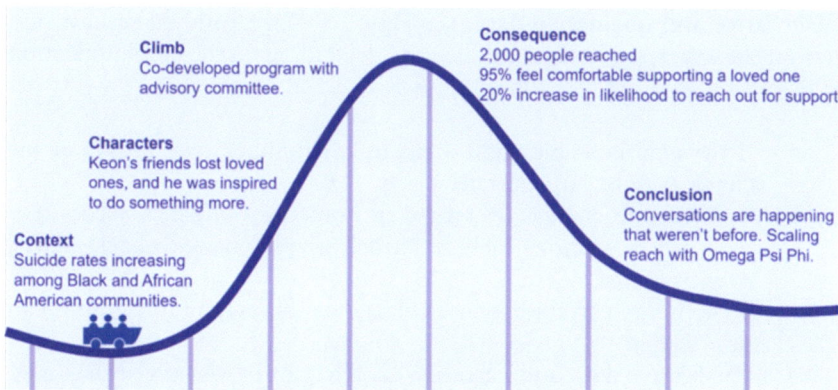

FIGURE 5-3 Crafting a narrative: Mapping data storytelling to a classic story arc using context, characters, climb, consequence, and conclusion.
SOURCE: Presented by Corbin Standley on April 29, 2025; American Foundation for Suicide Prevention.

to scale the reach of *L.E.T.S. Save Lives* through the Omega Psi Phi fraternity and historically Black colleges and universities throughout the country, extending its impact to new communities.

Building on Niederdeppe's presentation, Standley turned to the question of how to visualize the impact of a data story and effectively communicate it across different platforms and formats. While researchers often default to traditional outputs such as reports and slide shows, he encouraged participants to consider a broader range of formats that can be integrated into communication strategies from the beginning. These might include handouts, posters, data displays, social media graphics, and other materials tailored to the target audience and context.

Standley shared a few examples of real-world data visualizations,[1] as well as illustrations of a wide range of visualization options for both

---

[1] Examples included the Who Was Involved visualization in the "Impact Spotlight" for the 2023 International Survivors of Suicide Loss Day, available at https://www.datocms-assets.com/12810/1732043814-14842_afsp_impact_spotlight_issue3_m1.pdf; and a social media graphic shared on the AFSP Instagram page, viewable at https://www.instagram.com/p/DA59XVct-wA/?img_index=1

As an aside, Standley drew particular attention to the Instagram graphic, which reflects results from an annual Harris Poll commissioned by the National Action Alliance for Suicide Prevention and the Suicide Prevention Resource Center. According to the 2024 survey, 91 percent of U.S. adults believe suicide can be prevented at least some of the time, a notable increase since the survey began in 2015. Standley framed this shift as evidence of changing public attitudes, echoing earlier comments by Quinlan, and a testament to the collective efforts of those working in suicide prevention at the community and societal levels.

quantitative and qualitative data (see Figure 5-4). He offered several suggestions of how specific tools can be used depending on the communication goal:

- If the goal is to highlight a single key number, icon arrays or pie charts may be appropriate.
- To illustrate change over time or compare outcomes across two time points, options include barbell graphs, back-to-back charts, or histograms.
- To compare variables, scatter plots, heat maps, and line graphs can be effective.
- Qualitative data and narrative content can be visualized meaningfully using pull quotes, images, icon arrays, Venn diagrams, timelines, social network mapping, sentiment gauges, journey mapping, and storyboarding.

Standley highlighted storyboarding as a particularly valuable technique that allows researchers to align the logic model with the theory of action in crafting a story. He also cited quote graphics, used strategically on social media platforms, as a simple yet powerful tool to share themes in ways that resonate with audiences. He encouraged workshop attendees to explore Stephanie Evergreen's (2019) work on how evaluators and researchers can improve the presentation of findings through appropriate illustration selection.

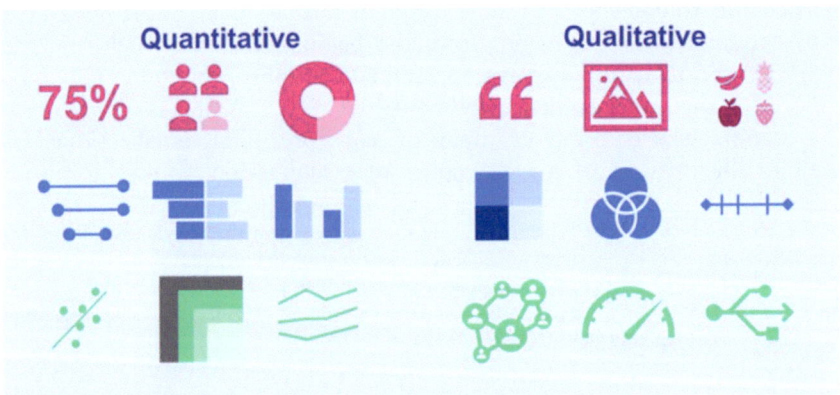

FIGURE 5-4 Types of visualization: Examples of tools to communicate quantitative and qualitative data.
SOURCES: Presented by Corbin Standley on April 29, 2025; American Foundation for Suicide Prevention; Evergreen (2019).

To illustrate how to improve the effectiveness and clarity of data visualizations, Standley next showcased a "before and after" example from the AFSP flagship program *Talk Saves Lives* (see Figure 5-5). He noted that the bar graph on the left leaves it up to the audience to interpret that the takeaway message is participation in the program increased over the last several years. The line graph on the right outlines the exact numbers and provides the takeaway in the graph title—participation in *Talk Saves Lives* has increased by over two times since 2022.

Standley reiterated the importance of selecting visualization tools that offer both clarity and meaningful interpretation, drawing on participant reflections shared AFSP's *International Survivors of Suicide Program* to illustrate this point (see Figure 5-6). In the word cloud example on the left, we can see that participants used terms such as *hope, healing,* and *connection* appear prominently, but the visualization offers little insight into what those words actually meant to participants. The thematic quote panel on the right provides that missing context by presenting direct quotes that reflect shared experiences and emotions—for example, the sense of connection and understanding that arises from being among others who understand the unique grief of suicide loss. These survivor voices tell a more powerful story than a word cloud alone can convey.

Standley concluded by emphasizing that this example illustrates why visual storytelling should be planned from the outset. Building visualizations into the broader dissemination strategy can ensure findings are not only seen but understood in ways that resonate with the intended audience.

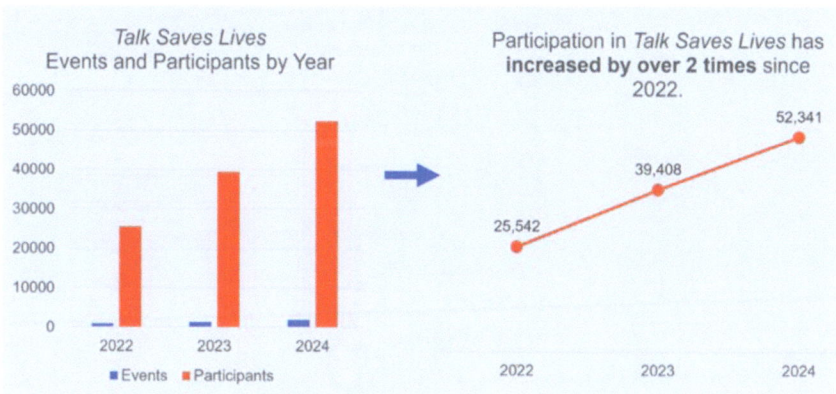

FIGURE 5-5 Quantitative "before and after".
SOURCE: Presented by Corbin Standley on April 29, 2025; American Foundation for Suicide Prevention; American Foundation for Suicide Prevention (2024).

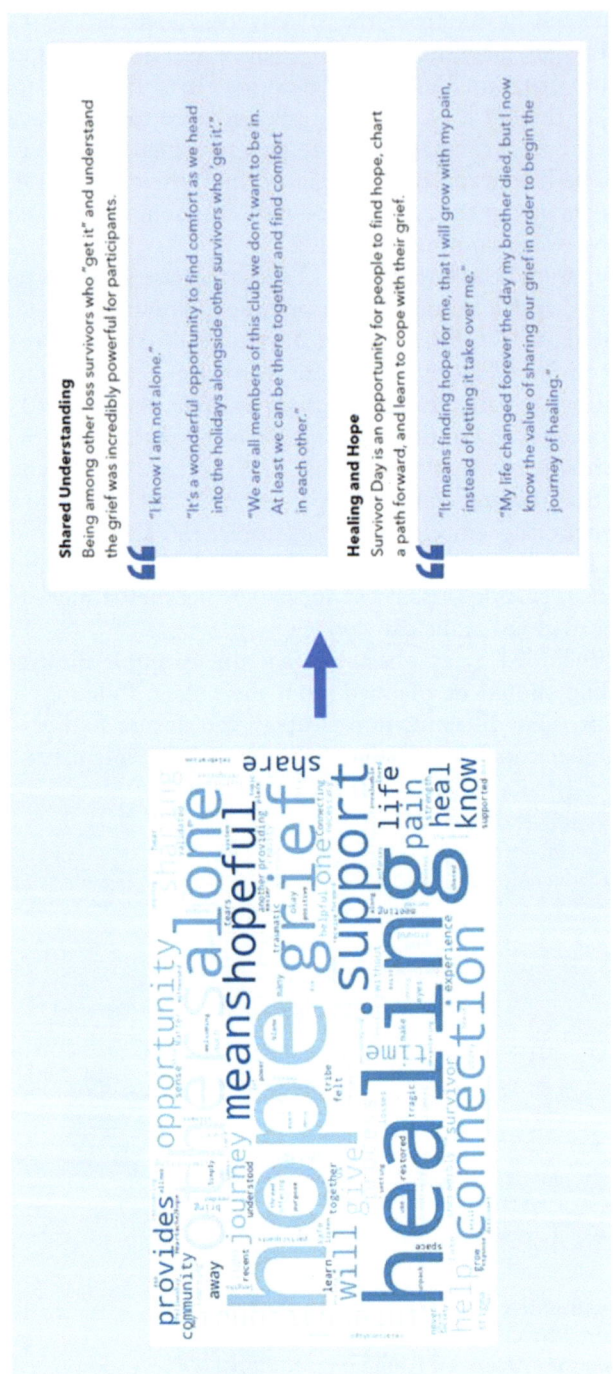

FIGURE 5-6 Qualitative "before and after".
SOURCE: Presented by Corbin Standley on April 29, 2025; American Foundation for Suicide Prevention (2024).

PANEL DISCUSSION AND AUDIENCE Q&A

Following Niederdeppe's and Standley's presentations, Mary Cwik (Johns Hopkins University), Novalene Alsenay Goklish (Johns Hopkins University, Brandi Jancaitis (Virginia Department of Veterans Services), Richard McKeon (SAMHSA), and Itzhak Yanovitzky (Rutgers University) joined them for the moderated panel discussion. Bernice Pescosolido (Indiana University; member, workshop planning committee) served as the moderator for this discussion. Panelists responded to guiding questions on the following topics: tailoring communication to different audiences, evaluating communication strategies, and sharing academic literature effectively.

Tailoring Communication to Different Audiences

Pescosolido began the moderated discussion by noting that this is a uniquely promising moment for public engagement, citing recent data from a representative sample in Indiana, where more than 90 percent of respondents—across a politically conservative state—expressed support for school-based mental health and suicide prevention programming. This surprising level of consensus, she said, reflects a shift in public attitudes and underscores the importance of thoughtful, inclusive communication strategies. She then invited the panelists to share examples of best practices for tailoring communication efforts and addressing the expectations of different communities, particularly in crafting messages that help audiences feel included.

Standley responded that one key focus for AFSP is the continuum of impact. Their work is trying to move individuals and the broader public from awareness to behavior change. However, he acknowledged that it can be difficult to communicate to funders, policymakers, and other stakeholders that a one-year intervention will not necessarily demonstrate measurable reductions in suicide rates at the community level.

Echoing earlier remarks by Kristen Quinlan, Standley pointed to indicators of progress, such as increased knowledge and awareness, reduced stigma and negative attitudes around suicide prevention, greater openness to discussing suicide and mental health, and growing willingness to reach out—either to support loved ones and friends who may be struggling or to seek help oneself.

Setting realistic expectations for evaluation, he added, requires recognizing that behavior change is complicated. Multiple elements must align to achieve behavior change, including awareness, knowledge, and attitude shifts, and the development of intent to change, Standley continued. How long the process of behavior change takes will vary depending on the community, the intervention, funding level, and the program's sustainability.

Communicating clearly about behavior change while tailoring language to the audience is important for getting people on the same page.

Yanovitzky raised the distinction between tailoring and targeting. Targeting, he explained, involves trying to engage a homogenous group of people, while tailoring involves trying to make a message more relatable. The goal is engagement, not dissemination, he said. To develop tailored messaging, the first step is clarifying the communication goal, Yanovitzky stressed. The goal might be to increase knowledge, to persuade, or to guide people in navigating action, as in cases where people are already motivated to act but are not sure how to proceed. Determining the nature of the underlying communication problem or opportunity is essential, Yanovitzky noted, as different problems and opportunities call for the application of different strategies.

Tailoring should be grounded in data about the target audience—not just demographic data, which he cautioned against over-reliance on, but deeper insights into beliefs, attitudes, knowledge, and values. As an example, he referenced Pescosolido's account of recent survey findings showing broad support for youth mental health programming in Indiana, noting that other survey data suggest support becomes more conditional when parents are asked specifically whether they would consent to depression screening for their children. He explained that concerns may differ across communities—for instance, some parents may worry about stigma in school settings, while others may have questions about how to access follow-up care. These nuances, he explained, underscore why audience research is essential to effective tailoring. It allows communicators to align goals, identify the right audiences, and understand where those audiences are—both geographically and in terms of readiness to act.

Niederdeppe emphasized the importance of engaging communities from the very beginning of program design and development. He noted that the people most interested in the results of an intervention are those who were involved in its origin, development, design, and implementation. One of the most effective ways to understand the values and needs of an audience, he suggested, is to collaborate with them from the outset in developing interventions. This ensures the intervention reflects the community's interests, goals, and conditions at the forefront, and builds a natural audience for communicating results. While it is not always possible to have a personal conversation with every potential stakeholder, Niederdeppe reiterated a point made earlier in the session: incorporating communication strategy into the earliest stages of intervention planning—particularly by involving community partners—can help ensure that dissemination efforts are aligned, meaningful, and impactful.

Jancaitis underscored the importance of understanding the audience and directly engaging with the military-connected community through focus groups, survey, and lessons learned. She illustrated this with an example of her work with the Virginia State Department of Behavioral Health on marketing for 988 in Virginia. Because there was not enough time to convene a formal focus group, she relied on her team—more than half of whom were military connected—to serve as an informal review panel. Their input quickly surfaced a critical issue that the contracted marketing firm had missed. For instance, they flagged an image of a 988-responder sitting in a cubicle in an open bay behind her, raising immediate concerns about data privacy and the perception of confidentiality.

Jancaitis added that using stock images can present a particular challenge in this context. Visual details such as a popped collar, missing rank insignia, or inappropriate hairstyle can erode a message's credibility with military audiences. "It doesn't matter how long you took to craft that message," she said. "Nobody is reading it" if the imagery signals inauthenticity.

Jancaitis also discussed the disconnect that can arise around terminology. In clinical settings, the term "safety planning" is well understood and generally viewed as positive. But among some community members, it may instead trigger fears of hospitalization, loss of rights or benefits, or the inability to support one's family. She stressed the importance of taking messages directly to the communities they are intended to reach, to ensure they are interpreted as intended.

She concluded with a final cautionary example. While supporting a research effort, her team assumed that having university and institutional review board approval would be sufficient to ensure community participation in a survey. That assumption proved mistaken. Community members, she said, "deconstructed every element of the survey"—work that had taken months to develop. The lesson, she emphasized, was that involving the community from the outset could have prevented that breakdown entirely.

Cwik brought up that the Johns Hopkins Center for Indigenous Health shared results with the community in addition to journals and policymakers. To utilize this momentum, her team created a large in-person event where the community members could receive the information directly from the researchers, which, she suggested, is better than the community having to gather information from the website or opening a newsletter. Cwik also noted that they made this large in-person event a celebration of the study being successfully completed: there was food, cultural singing, dancing. This study she mentioned was an elder youth program, so there were also a panel of Elders who spoke about their involvement in the program. The Center where Cwik and Goklish work also prioritized the community's culture, having as much of the celebration as possible in Apache, with translations, as well as sharing pictures and stories about working with the Elders and how the program worked. The final thing she mentioned was that, in an effort to express data in a creative way, one of the staff members took qualitative data from the study and created a painting of a cottonwood tree. The staff member then told an Apache story about the cottonwood tree that was related to the data gathered, which ended up being culturally congruent data.

Goklish continued discussing staff creatively discussing data by saying that having the parents and students see that their Elders were having a positive impact on the students. The data reflected this, showing that student's self-esteem increased as well as their connection to tradition and culture. She went on to discuss that having meetings to go over curriculum and allowing the Elders to go into the schools to teach had an impact immediately, but also that a continued loop of input from the Elders, the community, and feedback to the Elders ensures that the results and impact are felt both within the community and with the staff at the schools.

Evaluating Communication Strategies

Pescosolido asked how programs have approached evaluating their communication strategies. McKeon said, in terms of communication strategies, his team invested in trying to do focused research to get feedback from demographic groups who are at greater risk as well as a group of people who had a history of lived experience around suicide (in terms of a history of suicidal thoughts and attempts). The feedback around these focus groups (for example, one subgroup was concerned about if police would be sent/would someone end up hospitalized?) helped craft messaging to connect with the community and ease any fears.

Yanovitzky chimed in, stating that it is important to consider how communication strategies are aligned with underlying processes of change. He went on to say that, to influence policymaking, the communicator must respect the underlying process by which policymaking occurs. Yanovitzky stated, "having [a] communication strategy focus not on why, but [on] what can you expect to happen when you communicate with your audience would go a long way in terms of influencing behaviors." Communicators must respect the audience and the underlying process.

Niederdeppe added an important series of questions: why are the researchers evaluating communication? Is it to demonstrate benefit to a funder so that there are additional resources? That sort of evaluation, he said, demands a certain level of rigor and investment. Niederdeppe went on to ask, "how can we do this better?" He stated that a lot of organizations engage in modest, light experimentation and a-b testing. Niederdeppe recognized that while it is not the same level of rigor typically associated with peer-reviewed evidence that would justify a large investment, it does give information in real time that can inform practice.

Sharing Academic Literature Effectively

Pescosolido mentioned that academic publications don't always disseminate in a way that researchers would like, and asked what are ways that program developers and evaluators share academic literature in a more effective way? Before turning this question over to the panel, she shared her experience in that special issue publications seem to draw more academics and policymakers, as opposed to one-off articles.

Standley agreed with special issues being more attractive to academics and policymakers, but expanded, stating that publishing in a journal outside the field of suicide prevention, suicide research, and death studies is key, as publishing in those journals is "preaching to the choir." Instead, he suggested, consider publishing in journals like the *American Journal of Public Health, Journal of Public Health Management and Practice*, social work journals, or other journals that are adjacent, but not suicide specific. Standley went on to say that these other journals may be more open to other methodologies and suggested that a researcher might want to target methodological journals that publish participatory community engaged research or ones that publish mixed-methods and qualitative research.

Yanovitzky spoke to questions around implementation: how does someone navigate complex funding and legal environments? If someone was able to recruit and meet targets for clinical trials, especially in groups that are challenging to recruit, how did they do it? What did they do? How did they put their information out there? Yanovitzky said, "I want to encourage a lot of program relevant data, that maybe they're not measuring, maybe it's anecdotal. There's a lot of value to bring to the surface, so we can all benefit from that and move to [the] implementation side."

Pescosolido asked panelists to reflect on how grant programs might support grantees to evaluate local programs to facilitate that kind of publication. McKeon commented on communications to policymakers, that it is important to keep in mind the time frame for a policymaker is very different than other people, that they typically only have four to eight years, so they need to see more rapid change. He went on to say that when people are advocating for money, there is a tendency to talk about possibilities and, with suicide prevention's complexity and time-intensive nature, it is important to use a combination of metrics. McKeon suggested matching data with stories, utilizing compelling examples to make it clear why this initiative or intervention is important. He also noted that, for policymakers, it is important to focus on how your intervention will reduce suicide in the United States, rather than at a global level. For example, someone could say "these things reduced suicide in the White Mountain Apache community" or "this reduced suicide in the Henry Ford Health Care System" but maintain the goal of applying it in other communities.

Jancaitis spoke about the difficulties they are facing with their research grantees. She noted that it took a lot of time to work through academic approvals, hiring a team, working around student schedules, and their research is about to blossom into findings that can be used. However, she described challenges with figuring out how to package this research into a "toolkit-type digestible" and usable format, while keeping it completely free and accessible. She mentioned that a lot of research teams were unwilling to work with them since there are so many rules around what constitutes proprietary information. Jancaitis closed by saying that, as the funder, it was their responsibility to put in the proposal that their research should be free and accessible for grantees.

Audience Q&A

During the audience Q&A, several participants raised important questions about communication strategies, the role of credible messengers, and how to translate research findings into accessible tools for communities and policymakers. Panelists responded by reflecting on the challenges of crafting effective messaging, ensuring cultural relevance, and building trust with diverse audiences. The discussion also highlighted opportunities to align communication approaches with shared values and strategic partnerships.

Crafting Effective Messaging and Identifying Credible Messengers

Matthew Miller (VA Office of Suicide Prevention) commented that the general purposes for the communication might be agenda setting, persuasion, and coalition building, but that wasn't necessarily practice in federal government or how we think in public health or in suicide prevention: "We think in terms of realizing data, [we] don't think in terms of crafting a message," he stated. He went on to say that crafting a message could be viewed as manipulative but was curious on the panel's thoughts around the role of federal government, public health, suicide prevention, and crafting a message versus just releasing data.

Niederdeppe responded by first acknowledging that he did not mention in his presentation who should be doing the communication, which is central. He said that, in the last 10 to 15 years, there has been a steady erosion of trust in the federal government, public health, and in messaging in general. Niederdeppe emphasized that the federal government is not always best positioned to be the voice of communication; therefore, the question becomes: who is positioned to do that communication in a credible way, reaching the correct audience? Despite there being no one-size-fits-all solution, one thing communication science teaches, he said, is that an unexpected messenger can have a lot of value—for example, communicating in a way that defies expectations based on one's political orientation, which is connected to the coalition-building idea. Niederdeppe went on to explain that to identify people as credible messengers, the person must share a goal of implementing a policy or program, even if they have different reasoning but are willing to partner and are able to communicate resonantly and with values consistent with the group. He also mentioned that there is tremendous value to just having data for the purposes of planning and strategy, but that the researcher loses control once the data are put out into the public and can be mis- or re-interpreted in any number of ways, so decisions about when and how to release and frame data can be complicated.

Yanovitzky joined in on the conversation and stated that while he does not like to respond to questions before doing due diligence (which, in this context, means performing problem analysis, audience analysis, and pre-testing), his team has protocols to figuring out trusted communicators. He said that they do not assume who these communicators are, even still trusted voices like the CDC, he would rather find out for himself who these people are. Sometimes, Yanovitzky stated, he utilizes intermediaries or people from the community. He works with the National Alliance of Mental Illness and can get data from the researcher, use the data, and interpret the data, then tell stories about the data in terms of how it is making an impact on the community. "Here is the point. Data don't speak for themselves. If you don't speak for data then there's an information vacuum, and anybody can go and interpret the things. […] I can show a graph and manipulate the scale in a manner that makes a small change [look] like a big change. That's manipulation." Yanovitzky further stressed that, as long as there is the notion that there is an ethical standard (i.e., the third party looking at the report or if there are disclaimers about how data were interpreted), credibility is shown that way—however, there is no way to ensure credibility; rather, the target audience has the power to decide that. He went on to say that if someone wanted to be strategic, he suggested that they use scientific and robust tools for answering the questions who, how, and how we package information in a way that can facilitate comprehension.

Standley added that he often trains evaluators and researchers on how to share findings with policymakers, since it is very different than with community communication. One thing he suggested is called the "taxonomy of research use" which means understanding research evaluation data is one of many sources of information that policymakers are using to make decisions and that policymakers often use research in many different ways. Policymakers have two ways they use information: conceptual use (to shape the conversation and understand the scope of an issue) and instrumental use (to understand an issue well enough that they can propose legislation or support appropriations to target that issue). Standley noted that researchers and evaluators should act as mindful and honest information brokers when talking to policymakers, staffers, or others, especially in situations where data may be used tactically to support decisions that were made before the data were reviewed.

Leveraging Shared Values and Strategic Partnerships

Another audience member mentioned that, as a Staff Sergeant Parker Gordon Fox Suicide Prevention Grants Program awardee, they often leverage Standley's planning process. They mentioned that, though they present themselves as fairly liberal, they grew up on a farm hunting and fishing but also own a firearm and are a veteran. This audience member stated that they think the most effective route for communication around firearm safety is having specialists present the data around safety, rather than talking about policy to prevent ownership. They also mentioned that there are more opportunities when discussing safety this way, because they could partner with the National Rifle Association (NRA) since there are shared interests. This shared interest also serves as an avenue for the NRA, or similar partners, can present data to populations of interest on the researchers' behalf to garner interest and buy-in. The audience member said that they have tried this method and ground level testing in different populations which has been pretty successful.

REFERENCES

American Foundation for Suicide Prevention. (2024). Supporting those affected by suicide—the impact of International Survivors of Suicide Loss Day. *Impact Spotlight, 3*. https://www.datocms-assets.com/12810/1732043814-14842_afsp_impact_spotlight_issue3_m1.pdf

Evergreen, S. D. H. (2020). *Effective data visualization: The right chart for the right data* (2nd ed.). Sage.

McDonagh, L. K., Saunders, J. M., Cassell, J., Curtis, T., Bastaki, H., Hartney, T., & Rait, G. (2018). Application of the COM-B model to barriers and facilitators to chlamydia testing in general practice for young people and primary care practitioners: A systematic review. *Implementation Science, 13*(1), 130. https://doi.org/10.1186/s13012-018-0821-y

6

Reflections on Workshop Themes

Carrie Farmer (RAND Corporation) offered closing reflections at the end of the workshop. Drawing on key themes from across the sessions, she synthesized the discussions into four main areas of focus: program design, program implementation, program evaluation, and defining and communicating success. Her remarks highlighted recurring challenges, promising strategies, and considerations for strengthening suicide prevention grant programs.

PROGRAM DESIGN

Farmer highlighted that program design should reflect a clear understanding of the problem being addressed, with specific attention to how target populations are defined. She noted that some workshop participants stressed the need to be intentional about population definitions, including age ranges and population subgroups, to avoid overly broad or ambiguous eligibility criteria. Farmer also observed that there was considerable discussion about the challenge of balancing grant structure and flexibility. Grant programs must be structured enough to provide accountability and support implementation, while also being flexible enough to accommodate different organizational capacities and local contexts.

Another important discussion centered around the length of grants and sustainability of outcomes, Farmer added. She highlighted lessons learned from the Garrett Lee Smith program in particular related to the positive effects of longer-term funding on program impacts. In addition, activity timelines must incorporate sufficient time for outreach and marketing, evaluation, and communication and dissemination.

PROGRAM IMPLEMENTATION

On program implementation, Farmer underscored the importance of robust and responsive technical assistance. Many speakers throughout the workshop noted that implementation success often hinges on the availability of support tailored to grantees' needs and experience levels. Farmer pointed to the suggestion that technical assistance should begin early in the grant life cycle, ideally during the application phase, and continue throughout implementation. She also noted the value of peer-to-peer learning and structured opportunities for grantees to connect and share experiences. These interactions, she summarized, can foster a sense of community and support problem-solving.

Farmer reflected on the day's discussions related to data collection. There is a need for common data elements, as well as ensuring that the data collected are utilized and avoiding collection of data that are not needed. In addition, it is important to think through how to prioritize data that can be used at multiple levels, so they are beneficial to the program overall and also beneficial to individual grantees. Centralized data repositories may be helpful for achieving these goals.

PROGRAM EVALUATION

Farmer reflected on the workshop's discussion around evaluation, observing that evaluation was consistently described as most valuable when designed from the outset of a program. She emphasized that evaluation plans should be proportional to the scope and goals of the program, and that grantees should have access to guidance on how to integrate evaluation meaningfully. Multiple speakers suggested that funders consider offering tools such as standard logic model templates or curated lists of process and outcome measures to support grantees in this area.

DEFINING AND COMMUNICATING SUCCESS

Farmer addressed how success is defined and communicated within grant programs. She observed that several participants made the point that success should be defined in ways that are both rigorous and realistic, accounting for the community context and the maturity of the implementing organization. There are multiple audiences for this work, she added, and it is important to understand who the key audiences are; what their values and beliefs are; what programs want each audience to think, feel, or do; and what they need to know to change what they think, feel, or do. She highlighted a critical question about *who* should communicate program results—the answer depends on who the audience is and what you are trying to communicate. She also noted the suggestion that grantees should be encouraged to consider how they will share their work with others throughout the program period—not just through final reports, but also through storytelling, data dashboards, and other forms of dissemination. Communication, she added, is essential for encouraging broader learning and advancing the field. It is also important to evaluate the communication strategy to ensure the messaging is reaching the target populations, she stated.

CONCLUSION

Farmer concluded by acknowledging the range of experience represented across the workshop and the thoughtful discussion that emerged. Her synthesis reinforced the value of reflection, shared learning, and continued collaboration to strengthen the implementation and evaluation of suicide prevention programs.

Appendix A

Workshop Agenda

Workshop on Best Practices for Implementation and Evaluation of a Non-Clinical Community-Based Suicide Prevention Grants Program
April 29, 2025
National Academy of Sciences Historic Building
2101 Constitution Avenue, NW
Washington, DC

Lecture Room

And Via Webcast Accessible on the Event Page:
https://www.nationalacademies.org/event/44866_04-2025_best-practices-for-implementation-and-evaluation-of-a-suicide-prevention-grants-programs-a-workshop

AGENDA

(All Times Eastern Daylight Time)

9:00 am	**Welcome and Workshop Goals**
	Daniel J. Weiss, Board on Behavioral, Cognitive, and Sensory Sciences; National Academies of Sciences, Engineering, and Medicine

Carl A. Castro, Suzanne Dworak-Peck School of Social
Work, University of Southern California; Chair,
Workshop Planning Committee

9:15 am **Sponsor Perspective**
Matthew A. Miller, Office of Suicide Prevention,
Department of Veterans Affairs

9:25 am **Setting the Stage: Examples of Non-Clinical Community-Based Suicide Prevention Programs**

Session Introduction
Carl A. Castro, Suzanne Dworak-Peck School of Social
Work, University of Southern California; Chair,
Workshop Planning Committee

USAA Face the Fight
David Rozek, University of Texas Health Science Center at
San Antonio

Suicide Prevention and Opioid Addiction Services (SOS) Program
Brandi Jancaitis, Virginia Department of Veterans Services

White Mountain Apache Suicide Prevention Program
Mary Cwik, Johns Hopkins University
Novalene Alsenay Goklish, Johns Hopkins University

Garrett Lee Smith Memorial Suicide Prevention Program
SAHMSA Native Connections Grants Program
Richard McKeon, Substance Abuse and Mental Health
Services Administration (SAMHSA)

10:15 am **Best Practices for Program Development and Oversight and Grantee-Level Implementation and Performance Metrics**

Session Introduction
Daniel Friend, Mathematica; Member, Workshop Planning
Committee

The Public Health Approach and Comprehensive Suicide Prevention
Alex E. Crosby, Morehouse School of Medicine

APPENDIX A

Models for Effective Community Suicide Prevention
Elly Stout, EDC; Member, Workshop Planning Committee

Developing Logic Models for Evaluating Community-Based Interventions
Corbin Standley, American Foundation for Suicide Prevention

Comprehensive Technical Assistance to Support Program Outcomes
Carrie Farmer, RAND

Design of Actionable Dashboards for Supporting Program Implementation and Oversight
Itzhak Yanovitzky, Rutgers University

10:50 am   BREAK

11:00 am   Best Practices for Program Development & Oversight and Grantee-Level Implementation & Performance Metrics, continued

Moderated Panel Discussion, Part One: Lessons Learned from Examples of Non-Clinical Community-Based Suicide Prevention Programs

Moderator
Colin Walsh, Vanderbilt University; Member, Workshop Planning Committee

Panel Members
Mary Cwik, Johns Hopkins University
Novalene Alsenay Goklish, Johns Hopkins University
Brandi Jancaitis, Virginia Department of Veterans Services
Richard McKeon, SAMHSA
David Rozek, University of Texas Health Science Center at San Antonio

11:40 am   BREAK

11:45 am   Best Practices for Program Development and Oversight and Grantee-Level Implementation and Performance Metrics, continued

Moderated Panel Discussion, Part Two: Expert Insights on Program Development and Oversight and Grantee-Level Implementation and Performance Metrics

Moderator
Colin Walsh, Vanderbilt University; Member, Workshop Planning Committee

Panel Members
Ebony Akinsanya, CDC Foundation
Alex E. Crosby, Morehouse School of Medicine
Carrie Farmer, RAND
Elly Stout, EDC; Member, Workshop Planning Committee
Corbin Standley, American Foundation for Suicide Prevention
Christine Walrath, ICF
Itzhak Yanovitzky, Rutgers University

12:30 pm   Audience Q&A

12:45 pm   LUNCH

1:45 pm   Best Practices for Program Evaluation

Session Introduction
Diana Clarke, American Psychiatric Association; Member, Workshop Planning Committee

From Program Evaluation to Comprehensive, Community-Based Suicide Prevention Evaluation: Lessons Learned from the Field
Kristen Quinlan, EDC

Multi-site Community-Based Suicide Prevention Program Evaluation: An Example from the Field
Christine Walrath, ICF

Moderated Panel Discussion

Moderator
Diana Clarke, American Psychiatric Association; Member, Workshop Planning Committee

APPENDIX A   *111*

> **Panel Members**
> Mary Cwik, Johns Hopkins University
> Novalene Alsenay Goklish, Johns Hopkins University
> Brandi Jancaitis, Virginia Department of Veterans Services
> Richard McKeon, SAMHSA
> Tanha Patel, CDC Foundation
> Kristen Quinlan, EDC
> David Rozek, University of Texas Health Science Center at San Antonio
> Christine Walrath, ICF

2:55 pm   Audience Q&A

3:10 pm   BREAK

3:20 pm   Best Practices for Communicating Program Results

> *Session Introduction*
> Bernice Pescosolido, Indiana University Bloomington; Member, Workshop Planning Committee
>
> *Best Processes for Strategic Communication of Program Results*
> Jeff Niederdeppe, Cornell University
>
> *Data Storytelling: Best Practices for Communicating Impact*
> Corbin J. Standley, American Foundation for Suicide Prevention
>
> *Moderated Panel Discussion*
>
> **Moderator**
> Bernice Pescosolido, Indiana University Bloomington; Member, Workshop Planning Committee
>
> **Panel Members**
> Mary Cwik, Johns Hopkins University
> Novalene Alsenay Goklish, Johns Hopkins University
> Brandi Jancaitis, Virginia Department of Veterans Services
> Richard McKeon, SAMHSA
> Jeff Niederdeppe, Cornell University
> Corbin Standley, American Foundation for Suicide Prevention
> Itzhak Yanovitzky, Rutgers University

4:20 pm	**Audience Q&A**
4:35 pm	**BREAK**
4:40 pm	**Synthesis and Key Takeaways** Carrie Farmer, RAND
4:55 pm	**Closing Remarks** Carl Castro, Suzanne Dworak-Peck School of Social Work, University of Southern California; Chair, Workshop Planning Committee
5:00 pm	**ADJOURN WORKSHOP**

Appendix B

Biosketches

COMMITTEE MEMEBERS

CARL A. CASTRO (*Chair*) is currently professor and director of the Military and Veteran Programs at the Suzanne Dworak-Peck School of Social Work at the University of Southern California. He also serves as director of the University of Southern California-RAND Epstein Family Foundation Center for Veterans Policy Research. Castro served in the U.S. Army for more than 30 years, retiring at the rank of colonel. He participated in the Bosnia and Herzegovina and Kosovo Campaigns, Operation Northern Watch, and the Iraq War. Castro has chaired numerous NATO and international research groups, and he is currently co-chair of a NATO group exploring Military and Veteran Radicalization. He serves in an uncompensated capacity on the Cohen Veterans Network Scientific Advisory Board and as vice chair on the Board of Directors of the Greater Los Angeles Veterans Research and Education Foundation. Castro is a fellow of the America Psychological Association and the National Academy of Social Work and Social Welfare. His current research efforts are broad and include (a) the exploration of the military culture that leads to acceptance and integration of diverse groups; (b) understanding and ameliorating the effects of military trauma and stress, especially combat and deployment, on service members and their family; (c) the prevention of suicides and violence such as sexual assault and bullying; and (d) evaluating the process of transitioning into the military and transitioning from military service back to civilian life. Castro is a member of the National Academies of Sciences, Engineering, and Medicine's Committee on Evaluating the Effects of Opioids and Benzodiazepines on

All-Cause Mortality in Veterans and previously served on the Committee on Evaluation of Research Management by Department of Defense Congressionally Directed Medical Research Program.

DIANA E. CLARKE is the senior/managing director of research and senior epidemiologist/research statistician at the American Psychiatric Association. She is also an adjunct assistant professor in the Department of Mental Health at the Johns Hopkins Bloomberg School of Public Health. Clarke is president-elect for the International Academy of Suicide Research and has been an active member of the organization's board since 2020. She is also a certified mental health counselor. Clarke conducts research on the assessment and prevention of mental and substance use disorders with specific interest in understanding the underlying causes of suicide and suicidal behaviors. Her research also addresses the cultural context of suicide and suicidal behaviors and how cultural humility can lead to more informed prevention strategies. Clarke served on advisory panels for Patient-Centered Outcomes Research Institute (PCORI) and the executive committee of Friends of National Institute of Mental Health to help inform the future of funding for research on mental disorders including suicide. In addition, she has served as a grant reviewer for organizations such as PCORI and scientific officer for the Canadian Cancer Education and Research Network. She completed her graduate training in epidemiology at the University of Toronto and postdoctoral training in psychiatric epidemiology at Johns Hopkins Bloomberg School of Public Health.

DANIEL FRIEND is a principal researcher in Mathematica's Human Services division. He is also an adjunct faculty at two universities: the University of Illinois Chicago Public Health Department and the School of Psychology at DePaul University. Friend is an expert in behavioral health, behavior change theory, and implementations science. For over a decade, he has applied this knowledge to help the federal government—and others—develop, implement, and evaluate a range of health and human service programs. Currently, Friend is the principal investigator for the evaluation of the statewide California youth and behavioral health initiative and a project for the Administration for Children and Families aimed at improving healthy relationship and parenting services for Tribal/Indigenous communities. He holds an M.S. in psychology from the University of Oregon and a Ph.D. in public health and community health sciences from the University of Illinois at Chicago.

BERNICE A. PESCOSOLIDO is distinguished professor of sociology and director of the Irsay Institute for the Sociomedical Sciences at Indiana University. As a medical sociologist and network scientist, her research has focused on issues of suicide, mental illness and stigma. Drawing from classic work on suicide, Pescosolido has translated an early theory of group relationships into social network terms, developed direct and indirect measures of connectedness, and broken through data barriers in the study of completed suicide through harmonization of the U.S. Census' American Community Study and the Centers for Disease Control and Prevention's National Violent Death Reporting System. She has received career awards from the American Sociological Association and the American Public Health Association. An elected member of both the National Academy of Medicine (NAM) and the National Academy of Sciences, Pescosolido currently serves on NAM's Governing Council.

ELLYSON R. STOUT is the Education Development Center's (EDC's) U.S. director of community suicide prevention and serves as director of EDC's subcontract supporting the Substance Abuse and Mental Health Services Administration's 988 Communications Support Contract. She previously led the national Suicide Prevention Resource Center, and served as a program manager and behavior change communication director for PSI, an international public health social marketing company. Stout brings a background in global and U.S. public health, health communications, and behavioral health and suicide prevention. She has expertise in dissemination and implementation science and has worked for more than 17 years with states, tribes, communities, schools, and health systems to help fit bring national best practice guidance to their local context, culture, and assets. Stout is skilled in presenting complex information, providing coaching and consultation to diverse audiences, and working across a wide variety of settings, populations, and health outcomes. She is a Peter F. Krogh scholar and a Schweitzer fellow for life and received multiple academic honors in her studies. Stout is a member of the American Public Health Association and the International Association for Suicide Prevention and serves on several advisory groups and expert panels. Her undergraduate training is in international politics, and her graduate degree is in health communication.

COLIN G. WALSH joined the faculty at Vanderbilt University as assistant professor of biomedical informatics, medicine, and psychiatry and was later promoted to associate professor. His research includes machine learning to enable clinical decision support, scalable phenotyping with structured and unstructured clinical data, and public health informatics for preventive healthcare artificial intelligence. Walsh is a fellow of the American College of Medical Informatics, the International Academy of Health Sciences Informatics, and the American Medical Informatics Association. He received a degree in mechanical engineering from Princeton University and his medical degree from the University of Chicago. Walsh completed residency and chief residency in internal medicine at Columbia University Medical Center. Following residency, he received his primary professional degree in biomedical informatics in postdoctoral fellowship at Columbia University under research mentor George Hripcsak.

SPEAKERS

EBONY AKINSANYA is a distinguished public health leader with more than 25 years of experience in forging transformative partnerships, driving innovative program implementation, and optimizing resources to expand reach and impact. Her professional journey reflects a steadfast commitment to advancing public health outcomes through strategic thinking and operational excellence. As the Director of Non-Infectious Disease Programs at the CDC Foundation, Akinsanya leads a dynamic team in developing and promoting cutting-edge public health strategies and innovations. She is instrumental in fostering collaboration among internal and external stakeholders to scale initiatives, amplify impact, and support critical public health missions. Akinsanya's leadership spans several key areas, including evaluating veteran suicide prevention programs, enhancing maternal health outcomes, and empowering community-based organizations through capacity-building frameworks. In her previous roles, she thrived as an independent management consultant and public health privacy officer, spearheading initiatives to improve vocational rehabilitation services, ensure HIPAA compliance, and develop peer recovery coaching programs. Earlier in Akinsanya's career, she passionately advocated for HIV/AIDS communities, secured vital federal funding, and designed impactful health programs for underserved rural populations.

ALEX E. CROSBY currently serves as a professor in the Department of Community Health and Preventive Medicine at the Morehouse School of Medicine. He previously worked at the Centers for Disease Control and Prevention (CDC) for 30 years responding to numerous public health emergencies addressing suicide clusters, civil unrest, school-associated violence, sniper attacks, firearm-related injuries, and the response to hurricanes, Ebola, and Coronavirus. Crosby has authored or co-authored more than 125 publications. His work focuses on prevention of suicidal behavior, child maltreatment, intimate partner violence, interpersonal violence among adolescents, and assault injuries among minorities. Crosby graduated with a B.A. in chemistry from Fisk University, an M.D. from Howard University's College of Medicine, and an M.P.H. in health administration and management from Emory University's School of Public Health. He completed training in Family Medicine at Howard University Hospital, General Preventive Medicine and Public Health at Morehouse School of Medicine and the Georgia Division of Public Health, and epidemiology at the CDC's Epidemic Intelligence Service.

MARY F. CWIK is a licensed psychologist, associate director, and senior scientist at the Center for Indigenous Health at Johns Hopkins Bloomberg School of Public Health, with a joint appointment in psychiatry at the School of Medicine. For the past 20 years, she has focused on suicide, substance use, and trauma, particularly in addressing Native American mental health disparities. In partnership with the White Mountain Apache Tribe, Cwik's work has identified key risk and protective factors—including cultural identity—and supported interventions linked to reduced suicide rates. She is a Johns Hopkins distinguished alumna and has served on several local and national suicide prevention committees, including for the 988 Suicide and Crisis Lifeline. Cwik holds a B.A. in psychology and philosophy from Johns Hopkins University, a Ph.D. in child clinical psychology from Southern Illinois University, and completed a postdoctoral fellowship in child and adolescent psychiatry at Johns Hopkins.

CARRIE M. FARMER is codirector of the RAND Epstein Family Veterans Policy Research Institute, a senior policy researcher at RAND, and director of the RAND Health Care Quality Measurement and Improvement Program. For two decades, her research has focused on improving access to high-quality health care for veterans, service members, and their families. Farmer's work has included evaluations of the quality of U.S. Department of Veterans Affairs (VA) care, development of standards for high-quality mental health and traumatic brain injury care for veterans, systematic reviews of long-term outcomes for veterans with traumatic brain injury, state-based veteran needs assessments, and studies to assess the capacity of community providers to meet the health care needs of veterans. She has testified on access to VA health care before the U.S. Senate. Farmer holds a Ph.D. in health policy from Harvard University and a B.A. in psychobiology from Wellesley College.

NOVALENE ALSENAY GOKLISH is a member of the White Mountain Apache Tribe and has been an integral part of the Johns Hopkins University Center for Indigenous Health for more than 28 years. With her experience as a behavioral health interventionist, she has dedicated her career to improving the mental and physical well-being of her White Mountain Apache community. In Alsenay Goklish's current role as assistant scientist, she manages more than 15 mental and behavioral health initiatives focused on the health and resilience of Native American populations. At the beginning of her career, she began working with Native American pregnant teens, teaching prenatal wellness and parenting skills at Family Spirit. Today,

Family Spirit is recognized as an evidence-based model and is used in over 130 Native American and minority communities across the United States. In addition to her work on Family Spirit, Alsenay Goklish has contributed to a variety of behavioral health intervention projects aimed at addressing pressing issues within Native communities. These include programs focused on teen pregnancy prevention, youth entrepreneurship, and mental health support for at-risk youth. One of her key initiatives is the Celebrating Life Suicide Prevention Program, which provides critical support to community members who experienced binge substance use, non-suicidal self-injury, or suicidal thoughts or behaviors. Alsenay Goklish earned a B.S. in business management with an emphasis in community health education from the University of Phoenix, a M.S. in professional counseling from Grand Canyon University, and a Ph.D. in behavioral health from Arizona State University.

BRANDI JANCAITIS currently serves as the director of the Virginia Veteran and Family Support (VVFS) Program at the Virginia Department of Veterans Services (VDVS). VVFS is a statewide program that provides peer and family support and behavioral health and supportive services linkages to military service members, veterans, and their families. Also, in her current role with VVFS, Jancaitis oversees the Suicide Prevention and Opioid Addiction Services community and research grant program team. She also leads regional and statewide suicide prevention efforts for military and veterans including the Richmond Mayor's Suicide Prevention Challenge and statewide Governor's Suicide Prevention Challenge teams. Jancaitis also served as the director of housing development for veterans for VDVS and worked on the statewide effort to reach the functional end to veteran homelessness in Virginia. At the Virginia Department of Behavioral Health and Developmental Services, she served as the first Military and Veterans Affairs director and helped enhance treatment and supportive services in the public mental health system. Jancaitis is a graduate of Virginia Tech and Virginia Commonwealth University, an Army veteran spouse, and mother of three.

RICHARD McKEON is currently Senior Advisor in the Substance Abuse and Mental Health Services Administration 988 and Crisis Office after serving for 12 years as chief for the Suicide Prevention Branch in the Center for Mental Health Services where he oversaw all branch suicide prevention activities, including the Garrett Lee Smith State/Tribal Youth Suicide Prevention, and Campus Suicide Prevention grant programs, the Zero Suicide initiative, the Suicide Prevention Resource Center, and the Native Connections program. He has long worked with the National Suicide Prevention Lifeline, including establishing the foundation for 988 as the national suicide prevention number. Previously, McKeon was appointed by the Secretary of Veterans Affairs to the Secretary's Blue Ribbon Work Group on Suicide Prevention and later appointed by the Secretary of Defense to the Department of Defense Task Force on Suicide Prevention in the Military. He served on the National Action Alliance for Suicide Prevention Task Force that revised the 2012 National Strategy for Suicide Prevention and the U.S. Department of Health and Human Services project management team coordinating the 2024 revision of the U.S. National Strategy for Suicide Prevention. He also participated in the development of the World Health Organization's first World Suicide Prevention Report. McKeon has spent most of his career working in community mental health, including 11 years as director of a psychiatric emergency service and four years as associate administrator/clinical director of a hospital-based community mental health center in Newton, New Jersey. He was awarded an American Psychological Association Congressional Fellowship and worked in the United States Senate for Sen. Paul Wellstone, covering health and mental health policy issues. McKeon was also awarded the American Association for Suicidology Dublin Award for Lifetime Achievement in Suicide Prevention and was a finalist for the Samuel J. Heyman Service to America Medal for his contribution to the establishment of 988 as the new U.S. national suicide prevention and mental health crisis number. He spent five years on the board of the American Association of Suicidology as clinical division director and has also served on the board of the Division of Clinical Psychology of the American Psychological Association. McKeon received an M.P.H. in health administration from Columbia University and a Ph.D. in clinical psychology from the University of Arizona.

MATTHEW MILLER is the executive director of the Office of Suicide Prevention (OSP) where he leads a team dedicated to the implementation and reinforcement of U.S. Department of Veterans Affairs' (VA's) top clinical priority: preventing veteran suicide. OSP engages a public health approach to suicide prevention, integrating evidenced-based community and clinical interventions, strategic planning, program operations, program evaluation, and crisis services through the Veterans Crisis Line (VCL). Under his leadership, the VCL became the world's largest and most efficient suicide crisis call center and in 2022, expanded their life-saving services by implementing Dial 988 then Press 1. Miller has a focus on leading-edge technology and pioneering suicide prevention ideas and solutions through efforts like Mission Daybreak. He fosters non-traditional collaborations, recognizing the value of diverse perspectives and partnerships in achieving the shared goal of saving lives. Miller leads the team from a perspective that everyone plays a role in preventing veteran suicide. He began his VA career as the chief of mental health at Aleda E. Lutz VA Medical Center in Saginaw, Michigan, where he later became the deputy chief of staff. Miller was responsible for overseeing outpatient mental health operations for all service members and dependents within the installation community. In addition, he was head of the installation's suicide prevention, alcohol and drug demand reduction, critical incident response, and family advocacy programs. He is an Air Force Veteran. Miller received an M.P.H. from the University of Michigan and Ph.D. from Michigan State University. He completed his professional residency in clinical psychology at Wright-Patterson Air Force Base Medical Center and served as the chief of mental health at a Joint Services Pilot Training Wing.

JEFF NIEDERDEPPE is senior associate dean of faculty development in the Jeb E. Brooks School of Public Policy and the Liberty Hyde Bailey professor of communication and public policy at Cornell University. He is founding co-director of the Collaborative on Media and Messaging for Health and Social Policy (commhsp.org) and co-director of the Cornell Center for Health Equity. Niederdeppe's research examines the design and impact of media campaigns, strategic messages, news coverage, and social media content in shaping health behavior and social policy. He has published more than 220 peer-reviewed articles in communication, public health, health policy, and medicine journals, and his work has been funded in recent years by the National Institutes of Health, National Science Foundation, and Robert Wood Johnson Foundation. Niederdeppe was elected as a fellow of the International Communication Association. He serves on the editorial boards for seven journals in communication and public health. Niederdeppe currently serves on the Food and Nutrition Board of the National Academies, is a member of the consensus committee for a forthcoming National Academies report on Understanding Breastfeeding Promotion, Initiation and Support Across the United States, and previously served on the consensus committee for a 2018 National Academies report on Getting to Zero Alcohol-Impaired Driving Fatalities: A Comprehensive Approach to a Persistent Problem.

TANHA PATEL is a nationally recognized expert in public health evaluation with over 15 years of experience designing and implementing evaluations of community-based and systems-level initiatives. She currently serves as a senior technical advisor at the CDC Foundation, where she leads national evaluation efforts focused on maternal and infant health, veteran suicide prevention, and evaluation capacity-building among community-based organizations. Patel has developed and implemented evaluation toolkits, facilitated national trainings, and supported the strategic use of data for more than 100 health care and public health professionals. Her leadership has advanced the understanding of how non-clinical, community-rooted programs contribute to suicide prevention and overall public health impact. Patel has administered mini-grants and provided individualized technical assistance to veteran-serving organizations to strengthen their capacity to document outcomes and build sustainable, evidence-informed non-clinical suicide prevention programs. Previously, she led evaluation efforts at the University of North Carolina and Wake Forest School of Medicine, where she guided multi-million-dollar National Institutes of Health–funded programs in translational research and learning health system transformation. Patel's work has been published in leading journals including *Learning Health Systems* and the *Journal of Clinical and Translational Science*. She brings a deep commitment to translating evaluation findings into actionable strategies that enhance the effectiveness of comprehensive suicide prevention efforts.

KRISTEN QUINLAN is a senior research scientist at the Education Development Center, where she serves as a senior research advisor for the National Action Alliance for Suicide Prevention. In this role, she supports the Progress, Accountability, and Data Advisory Group, which is working to develop and launch a framework for tracking progress on the *National Strategy for Suicide Prevention*. Working closely with public and private sector partners, Quinlan is currently drafting the National Strategy's Theory of Change Framework. This role demands proficiency in developing complex, nested logic models that reflect the functioning of a national system, a comprehensive understanding of the landscape of suicide prevention across the nation, effective leadership in engaging cross-agency and cross-sector partners, and a strong familiarity with the U.S. Department of Health and Human Services and other national surveillance systems. Throughout her career, Quinlan has been dedicated to enhancing evaluation capacity within grassroots agencies, communities, and states. As the director of evaluation for the Substance Abuse and Mental Health Services Administration–funded Suicide Prevention Technical Assistance Center, she evaluates the operational effectiveness of the national center and supports grantees in their evaluation-related needs. Quinlan is deeply committed to injury control and prevention, co-founding the Intersectional Council Workgroup for Suicide Prevention in the American Public Health Association. This initiative aims to engage all 32 member sections in promoting the importance of public health approaches to suicide and violence prevention. Quinlan has served as adjunct faculty for the University of Rhode Island and Rhode Island College, teaching in the Psychology and Women's Studies Departments. She has more than 15 years of experience in working in public health. Quinlan received a Ph.D. from the University of Rhode Island in behavioral science with a focus on research methods.

DAVID C. ROZEK is a board-certified clinical psychologist and associate professor in the Department of Psychiatry and Behavioral Sciences at the

University of Texas Health Science Center at San Antonio. He serves as the director of strategy and evaluation for the STRONG STAR Training Initiative and the Senior Scientific Advisor for *Face the Fight*, a national suicide prevention initiative focused on scaling evidence-based interventions for veterans. Rozek's research and clinical work focus on cognitive and behavioral therapies for suicide, PTSD, and depression, with a strong emphasis on increasing access to effective care through real-world implementation strategies. His work has been funded by the National Institutes of Health, Department of Defense, Boeing Corporation, USAA, and state and local agencies to advance suicide prevention and trauma recovery efforts across diverse populations, including military personnel, first responders, and high-risk civilians. Rozek has published over 40 peer-reviewed scientific articles and delivered more than 50 invited talks and conference presentations. His trainings have reached thousands of mental health professionals, peer specialists, and public safety personnel both nationally and internationally. He is committed to bridging the gap between research and practice to improve mental health outcomes in underserved and high-risk communities. Rozek received a Ph.D. in clinical psychology from the University of Notre Dame, completed his residency at the Orlando Veterans Affairs Medical Center, and a postdoctoral fellowship in clinical neuroscience at the University of Utah.

CORBIN J. STANDLEY is a community psychologist and researcher with more than a decade of experience in research, evaluation, and policy. His career has focused on public health and community-level approaches to suicide prevention through capacity-building, equitable systems change, and policy change. Standley has published numerous research articles and book chapters and has presented his research at multiple national and international conferences. As the senior director of impact communication and continuous improvement at American Foundation for Suicide Prevention (AFSP), he leads the continuous improvement and evaluation of AFSP and partnership programs and initiatives; drives impact communication efforts to disseminate AFSP's reach and impact; and drives organizational learning through needs assessments, continuous improvement approaches, and special evaluation initiatives. Standley's dedication to community-engaged scholarship earned him the American Association of Suicidology's Citizen Scientist Award and multiple nominations for Forbes 30 Under 30 for Science. He has also used his research to inform policy work in providing testimony, helping to draft legislation, and working with legislators to prevent suicide. These efforts earned Standley the Sandy Martin Grassroots Field Advocate for the Year Award from AFSP. His commitment to amplifying and empowering voices in evaluation earned him an American Evaluation Association President's Award. He earned a B.S. in psychology from

Weber State University, and an M.A. and Ph.D. in ecological-community psychology from Michigan State University.

CHRISTINE WALRATH is a senior vice president and chief science officer in public health at ICF and brings more than 25 years of expertise in behavioral health research and community-based program evaluation. Her experience has been dedicated to understanding the patterns, characteristics, and outcomes of individuals at risk for suicidal behavior or experiencing mental illness, focusing on areas such as prevention and service system response, child traumatic stress, school-based mental health, co-occurring disorders, serious emotional disorders and mental illness, and engagement of individuals with lived experience. Walrath has supported the Substance Abuse and Mental Health Services Administration (SAMHSA) on numerous high-priority behavioral health initiatives, serving as principal investigator of large-scale, national evaluations of SAMHSA-funded programs, including the Garrett Lee Smith Youth Suicide Prevention Program, the Zero Suicide Program, and the 988 Lifeline and Crisis Services initiative. Her recent work includes designing and implementing multimodal, multilevel, and multisite approaches to data collection; developing instruments; analyzing large-scale primary and extant behavioral health data; using data to drive program and practice; providing training and technical assistance in the areas of data collection, management, and submission; and disseminating research findings to diverse audiences. Walrath has a dual background in community psychology and public mental health and began her career at the Johns Hopkins Bloomberg School of Public Health, where she still holds an adjunct faculty position.

ITZHAK YANOVITZKY is professor of communication and professor of public health at Rutgers University. He is an expert in the areas of behavior change communication, translational research, and program evaluation. Yanovitzky's program of research explores effective mechanisms for communicating complex information to diverse audiences and improving use of evidence in health policymaking and practice settings. He has extensive experience partnering with collaborators across academic disciplines and sectors to address a range of public health problems, including most recent efforts to address the opioid epidemic and the rising toll of youth depression and suicide. Yanovitzky is past chair of the Health Communication Division of the International Communication Association and a past member of the National Academies of Science, Engineering, and Medicine's Standing Committee on Advancing Science Communication.

STAFF

SHARON BRITT is the program coordinator for the Board on Behavioral, Cognitive, and Sensory Sciences. She previously worked at Howard University Hospital as a program coordinator with the Graduate Medical Education Department. In this position, she managed the Orthopedic and Podiatric Surgery Residency program that prepares residents to succeed in their practice locations and specialties and provides high-quality care. Prior to Britt's position as the residency coordinator, she worked on several government contracts as a helpdesk manager and IT analyst. She graduated from Strayer University in Washington, D.C., with a bachelor's degree in business administration.

DANIEL J. WEISS is the director of the Board on Behavioral, Cognitive, and Sensory Sciences. Prior to assuming this role, he served as a professor of psychology and linguistics at The Pennsylvania University. Weiss's research focused on language acquisition and motor planning, using a comparative approach, measuring performance across human infants and adults as well as nonhuman primates. He graduated summa cum laude from the University of Maryland and completed his master's degree and Ph.D. in the Cognitive Brain and Behavior program at Harvard University. After finishing his Ph.D., Weiss was a postdoc for three years at the University of Rochester. He also recently served a term as the editor-in-chief for *Translational Issues in Psychological Science*.

TINA M. WINTERS is a program officer with the Board on Behavioral, Cognitive, and Sensory Sciences (BBCSS) at the National Academies of Sciences, Engineering, and Medicine (National Academies). She has worked on many consensus studies and other projects on topics including leveraging behavioral science to reduce the impact of dementia, factors that bear on the quality and success of scientific research, influences on aging, program evaluation, and learning across the lifespan. Prior to joining BBCSS, Winters's work at the National Academies centered on studies and other activities related to K–16 science and mathematics education, educational assessment, and education research.